Joseph and Lois Bird advocate a revolutionary approach to rearing children—*common sense:*

About goals and achievement: "The (educational) goals which can be realistically set are considerably higher than most parents seem to realize. We have heard so many warnings about 'pushing' the child, and the supposedly dreadful things which can happen to children who 'over-achieve.' With educators and popular child 'experts' so strongly dedicated to the comfort of mediocrity, this is to be expected."

About corporal punishment: "There is no evidence a spanking is any more harmful psychologically than physically."

About drugs: "If your teenage son or daughter is 'average,' he or she has already experimented with drugs, or will soon. Even with a considerable degree of awareness and control, we may not prevent it. If we attempt to ignore it, we encourage it."

About the "communication gap": "Communication is always a two-way street or it isn't communication. Parents can become fixated on 'drawing the child out' and overlook the importance of sharing. He wants to know about your world. You both want and *need* to know about his."

About sex: "How much information should the child be given and at what age? The fact that this question is asked at all probably attests to the anxiety we parents feel in the matter of sex . . . There should be no age at which *truth* and knowledge are withheld."

Power to the Parents!

Power to the Parents!

A Common-Sense Psychology
of Child Raising for the '70s

Joseph and Lois Bird

IMAGE BOOKS

A Division of Doubleday & Company, Inc.
Garden City, New York
1974

Image Books edition
by special arrangement with Doubleday & Company, Inc.
Image Books edition published February, 1974

To: *Paul*
Ann
Susan
Kathleen
Joan
Stephen
Michael
Mary
Diane

We hope we have been able to say what
we have wanted to tell you. If we have,
it is because we have shared the joy and
privilege of living for a time with you, nine
truly remarkable and beautiful human beings.
And for this, we thank you.

CONTENTS

ileges . . . Verbal Punishment . . . United
Parental Front . . . Moralizing . . . Spanking . . . Basic Hints

Power to the Parents!

1

A LETTER
TO CONCERNED PARENTS

Dear Fellow Parents:

The parent with access to a bookstore or public library certainly does not lack assistance in child rearing. There are books in print on virtually every area of child development, ranging from the prenatal stage through the college, running the gantlet from toilet training to dating, thumb-sucking to new math. The conscientious parent who attempts to keep abreast of the accelerating literature would do well to take a speed-reading course. But of one thing we can be sure, we will not be left in the dark for want of advice from the experts. Add to the books the articles appearing in popular periodicals, and we will have no questions left unanswered.

In working one's way through the volumes of expertise, one might, nevertheless, come a cropper. There may be several answers to the same question. The experts are frequently at odds as to what is observed in a child and what, if anything, should be done about it. Child rearing is far from an exact science. Expert What's-His-Name tells you how to teach a four-year-old how to read, while expert Somebody-or-Other warns of the emotional dangers in teaching reading to a child before he is "ready." While one authority will advise giving only so much information as is necessary "at that age" when your child asks, "Where do babies come from?" another will map out a program of sex education designed to turn out classes of amateur sexologists in the elementary school.

We may decide to pick our expert and stick with him all the way. We may jump around from one to another, following Expert A for six months, Expert B for the following year, Expert C through that trying period in the second grade, and end up either throwing them all out with the broken plastic toys or becoming eclectic in our approach, with a potpourri of assorted advice from each, perhaps hopelessly confused and chronically guilty of knowingly going against the dicta of one or another of the authorities.

Even if we attempt to avoid the conflicts by selecting just a single text and following it with the strict adherence one might pay to a military manual, we will still be likely to run into difficulties. First of all, our five-year-old may not act very much like the five-year-old the expert describes. The differences, in fact, may seem greater than the similarities. The parent of several children who is even minimally observant cannot help being aware of how much each child is a distinct and somewhat unique human being, and that what may apply to quiet, thoughtful Jimmy at age seven will not fit active, boisterous Carl at the same age. They may have the same set of parents, but they weren't stamped out of a mold. Secondly, the circumstances and environment the expert describes or assumes may differ greatly from what exists in your home. Obviously, the six-year-old only child living in an apartment in the city with both parents employed outside the home lives in a world very different from that of the six-year-old who is the eldest of four and lives with his family on a farm.

More serious difficulties lie in the results of raising a child within the psychological framework of what is implied in nearly all the books on child rearing: that eight-year-old Billy or eleven-year-old Betty live in worlds in which they are the sole occupants. They inform their readers of the expected behavior of an eight-year-old, but aside from the usual comments on sibling rivalry, there is little or no attention paid to the context, the environment, in which he lives. He has parents, and his parents, the readers, are told how to best meet his physical and emotional needs, but one never gets the impression from the reading that the parents exist as anything other than functionaries whose sole purpose is to serve his needs. They are Father and Mother, but they are not a man and a woman, hopefully in love with each other, who have a life of their own which they share. He may have brothers and sisters, yet they seem to form only a sort of background against which he moves. Seldom is anything said about his responsibilities toward them. In other words, the entire focus in childrearing literature is on the individual child and his world. It is not directed toward how he can and should function as a member of a family.

Perhaps we can illustrate our point with a few examples. We will not identify the sources since they are no worse, although no better, than the average. In one widely read book on child behavior, the authors tell us that some three-year-olds enjoy wandering about the house late at night while the family sleeps, exploring places and things, perhaps getting something to eat from the refrigerator, and maybe sleeping the rest of the night on the living-room sofa. So far, so good. We agree there are some three-year-olds who might enjoy such nocturnal adventures, but the authors then go on to tell the concerned parents that this is really nothing to be concerned about. All the parents need do is to make sure the front and back doors are locked so the child can't wander out into the street. And put the knives and poisons out of reach. This may be normal expected behavior of the three-year-old, but what the experts don't tell us is the normal expected behavior of the three-year-old's mother the following morning as she cleans up the mess of spilled milk, sugar, breakfast cereal, and what-have-you, and tries to remove the lipstick he has used to decorate the living-room wall.

The same experts tell us that some three- and four-year-olds don't care to go right to sleep when they are put to bed at night. They prefer to have the light left on (they

are old enough, the writers tell us, to turn it out when
they are ready) and to play with their toys for a time until
they are sleepy. Nothing wrong here, they say; let the
child play if he wishes. Of course he may be cross and
whiny the next morning from lack of sleep but, well, no
matter; that's the parents' hang-up. They do, however,
concede the possibility of one problem: He may share a
bedroom with a year-and-a-half-old brother who may have
difficulty sleeping in the midst of these activities. Their
suggested solution: Provide the three-year-old with a private room. Just don't have a family the size of ours or, with
every child occupying a private room, you'll end up leas-
ing your home from Conrad Hilton.

Another authority calls our attention to a pair of opposite extreme problems faced by some second graders.
Some children at that stage, he says, will fall into the habit
of dawdling in the morning, never dressing in time, pro-
crastinating over breakfast, and consequently, repeatedly
getting to school after the bell rings. He suggests the parents handle the problem by talking to the teacher and
asking her if she can't arrange some little project or chore
at which he can assist her that would be fun for him for
fifteen or twenty minutes before school starts. This, hopefully, would motivate him to get to school on time! One
wonders if the teacher might not be motivated in a very
different direction.

The other problem second grader is almost compul-
sive in his punctuality. He is described as rising an hour
or two before the other members of the family and virtually drives them to distraction worrying that he will be
late for school, rushing through his breakfast (when he
isn't too upset to eat) and, in general, acting much like an
obsessive-compulsive neurotic. Our expert's suggested
means of coping with the problem is—are you ready?—to
place him in a school which has no rigid starting time and
no bells or buzzers, the idea being, of course, that he can't
be late if there is no set time he is expected to be there.

So much advice of this nature has been given that we

have come to expect that child rearing means adapting to the ever-changing needs and demands of the child.

Parents have understandably bought it—and how! Just this week we talked with the mother of a sixteen-year-old girl. She told us of their family, Father and Mother, the daughter, and two sons, twelve and eleven, going to the movies. First, the daughter refused to go ("I know you can't expect a teen-ager to want to go out with the family."), then went along only after the father exerted considerable pressure. When they got to the theatre, she declined the invitation to sit with them ("You know how kids are these days; they're embarrassed to be seen with their parents."). Like so many parents, she took for granted that this is the way adolescents *are*, nothing abnormal about it, and nothing which could be avoided. "Man, I just want to be left alone. I just want to do my *own thing*."

Anything unusual or in the least unexpected in that? Of course not. The child-rearing experts have told us how the eight-year-old does his "thing," and how we shouldn't be concerned when the three-year-old is doing his "thing" as he goes on his late-night strolls. And the second grader for whom the teacher rearranges her before-school routine is only doing his "thing." So we not only provide him with a separate room, we construct for him a separate world. He not only ends up with the world on a string, he has his family tied in knots at the other end of that string.

Things have changed, and parents today do face problems, many of them serious, in raising their children. Those who are always ready to offer simplistic answers will try to persuade us to turn the clock back. The three R's and the little red schoolhouse held the promise of purity and godliness to those whose intellect is clouded by the distortions of nostalgia. A California educator-politician has called for a return of the portraits of Washington and Lincoln to the classrooms and daily recitation of the pledge of allegiance as a counterforce to the demise of patriotism in youth. He has followers, as those demigods with simple solutions to complex problems will always attract followers.

But there are no gimmicks, no psychological or educational clichés which will ease the responsibilities of parenthood. We can try to explain what happened and what is happening with children, but the explanations, even if some at least are valid, do not necessarily point the way to a solution. None of us is unaware that the structure of our society has changed from what it was in our childhood and the childhood of our parents. Families are more mobile. More are living in the cities and the cities are larger and more sprawling. Fathers hold jobs which call for more travel. They work at occupations which are more complex, more frustrating, and less personally rewarding. Women have taken headlong strides toward what they have called emancipation ("you've come a long way, baby") and have entered the labor market in force. Television has taken over the bulk of the families' leisure time. The divorce rate, use of drugs, and child suicides have all increased along with the family income and the average number of years of schooling. We fear the cities and look with disdain on suburbia. We buy homes with thirty-year mortgages, which we intend to sell in five or ten years, homes with two and three bathrooms, all of which stay cluttered, and two-car garages, which are so jam-packed with discarded items we can't get the second car, a station wagon, through the door. We brag of the quality of our children's school district without ever questioning whether the schools are teaching our children what we think they should learn. Then when the children get into trouble, start smoking pot, set fire to the school, or come home pregnant in junior high school, we start looking for reasons. Television, progressive education, the new affluence, sex, and the mass media. There's just got to be an answer there somewhere. Maybe rock 'n' roll music is causing the kids to turn to dope. Perhaps sex-education classes are leading to illegitimacy. And who knows, could it be the Saturday morning cartoons which are driving children to do in their parents with a bread knife? Someone once found a positive correlation between the production of Puerto Rican rum and the salaries of Presbyterian ministers in New England. Do you suppose one caused the other, perhaps that the parsons were secretly subsidized by the distilleries in Puerto Rico?

We have become educated (to what, we can't be sure) and psychologically sophisticated. Since the turn of the century, our psyche-social views have changed almost completely. There has been a growth of a new humanism, one which is seldom well defined, in which we speak more of a concern for our fellow man while at the same time finding rationales with which to excuse our lack of concern. First there was Freud. How could we be expected to assume responsibility for our actions if these actions were triggered by dark forces hidden deep within our Id, forces created and shaped by traumatic toilet training and a castrating mother? Freud, however, wasn't the villain. Humans can always be expected to seek an absolution without penance. The public found in Freud the forgiving confessor, perhaps a redeemer. In reading and misreading his *General Introduction to Psychoanalysis* (they seldom went further), they found a forgiveness for their failures, a hard-core determinism, almost a fatalism, which would explain away their foibles and indiscretions.

With the rejection of the rigid ethics of nineteenth-century Christianity with its concept of free will and its emphasis on personal responsibility, sin and boot-strap salvation, the pendulum stopped its swing toward the ultimate in the spiritually self-made man and began its swing in the opposite direction. The individual conscience gave way to such concepts as Jung's collective unconscious. The more esoteric and "deep," the more appealing. How could one struggle against life if life itself, as Rank told us, begins with the "birth trauma?" Could anyone hold the rapist responsible for his act when it became known that as an infant he witnessed the "primal scene?" And who would blame a husband for being irresponsible if the poor fellow is suffering a crippling rejection and resultant hostility toward women owing to abrupt weaning from Mommie's breast?

Life, we quickly learned, is not what you make of it; it is something which happens to you, something which sweeps over you, like a disease, like a wave washing over a rock. Psychological passivity became the game of living. We began to accept the notion that being *reactive* was more normal and healthy than being *active*. Now, the self-made man was seen as having a neurotic need for autonomy. The man with ambition was "overcompensating" for some feelings of inadequacy. The man of principle was scrupulous. If he accepted his own self-demands, he was "uptight." If he listened to the sound of his own drummer, he was a poor "team player."

Reactive statements crept into nearly every conversation: "She made me angry." "He turned me off." "I felt myself becoming defensive." "I didn't choose to have an affair; it just happened." "I screamed at my husband because the kids had been driving me up the wall." "It was the pressure at the office which made me lash out at her." "I couldn't help it; when he says things like that, I just see red." Everything a copout, a chain of buck-passing. Why do I shout at my daughter? Because I woke up with a headache. No choice involved. The headache *compelled* me to shout at my daughter.

Accepting our own buck-passing as an escape from freedom of choice and responsibility, we have set forth to teach it to our children. And they have learned it well.

At a workshop for school superintendents held at Columbia University, students were given the opportunity to voice their complaints. One girl claimed she became hooked on drugs because she had teachers who couldn't communicate with her. Said another, "I'm tired of adapting to schools; let the schools adapt to me." The students didn't speak of their own responsibilities, but one spoke for many in saying, "Schools have as much responsibility as parents in helping kids grow up to be healthy, happy, loving people."

Lawyers and social workers have pinned the blame for juvenile violence on broken homes, impoverished neighborhoods, and a lack of playgrounds. "Having no place to play but the streets, he turned to crime." It isn't solely the child of the slums who has been provided a copout. Clarence Darrow, the famed trial lawyer, argued in defense of the confessed killers Loeb and Leopold that the boys had been cursed with too *much* wealth. One college student told us he turned on with LSD to escape his "uptight religious background." Another said he took acid in a search for God. Fourth graders fail in school *because* they can't relate to their teachers. Teen-agers steal hubcaps *because* they can't communicate with their parents. And so it goes. The buck goes round and round and round.

Comes, however, the moment of truth, the facing of reality, the painful acceptance of the fact that that buck must eventually come to rest. Unless the lives of all concerned are to risk becoming a shambles, we as parents must accept the fact that the buck stops with us.

Whenever Mommie says she "couldn't resist" buying the new hat which overdrew the checking account and Daddy says he "couldn't control" his temper when he flew into a rage, they are teaching their children to cop out. Behavior which we might find intolerable in our children is accepted as uncontrollable in ourselves. Little wonder that the nine-year-old when asked why he broke all the dishes in the cupboard answered, "I couldn't help it; I was frustrated."

Parents claim they fear their children, especially their teen-agers, and well they might. They say that the children show them no "respect." But what is meant by respect, and why do parents feel it is owed them? They complain that their offspring—and most youth of today—are irresponsible. They may be right, but how do they define "responsible" and "irresponsible" and how do they teach responsibility?

Parents say they can't predict what their child may do next ("he's always into something"). Often, the child is in as great a state of confusion and even more vulnerable. He can't predict what the parent may do next. His best bet may be that his parents will act consistently inconsistent.

We parents today are under siege. We are pressured from every side. As Jimmy Durante says, "Everybody wants ta get inta the act"—of raising our children. Schoolteachers and scout masters, maiden aunts and ministers, all tell us what we should do *with* our children, *for* our children, and *to* our children. This is not, however, another copout. Nothing compels us to follow the dictates of the pressure groups or self-styled authorities. We cannot blame the advice givers if we are only too willing and eager to sit at the foot of every passing oracle. That J. Edgar Hoover, an elderly bachelor law-enforcement officer, is willing to make public his views on the causes and cures of child misbehavior should surprise no one, but when we discover parents looking to Mr. Hoover for advice on child rearing, we may be understandably dismayed at the psychological straws at which so many of us are ready to grab.

If only someone would provide a simple, painless method of child rearing, one guaranteed to bring success without strain or thought or personal responsibility, we might beat a path to his door. But no one has come up with any such method. Many parents are attempting to do what they feel is the next best thing: Follow everyone and anyone. Flow with the tide. Go along with the community.

So what's wrong with that? Assuming we can get all members of the community to agree on what they want for their children, perhaps we can raise them in some sort of psychological kibbutz. If that is what you feel is best, you have our blessings. We believe, however, that you want something else for your child. We know we do. Furthermore, we are willing to "go along" with the current practices of the community only when we find such practices, and the resultant community, *healthy*. And far too much of the time, what we observe today is irresponsible, destructive, unhappy, and unhealthy.

Conforming to the views of the "experts" and the current child-rearing practices of the society may seem the easiest way. Conformity always seems easier than bucking the tide. But it comes with a price. We may have some glimmer of the price if our children have already become "problems," but there are other prices as well of which we may be unaware. To cite just a few:

1. *Anxiety*. Attempted conformity leads to feelings of vulnerability. If we choose to follow the group, any deviation from the group practices will leave us open to criticism and attack—both from the group members and from our children. If we have followed the neighbors in the past, we may have little defense against the argument "All the other kids' parents let them do such and so," and few means with which to counter the mother down the block who says, "The other mothers and I have talked it over and we think . . ." Vulnerability produces anxiety, a feeling of impending doom. It can become a terrible price.

2. *Hostility*. We cannot conform to a society which encourages egocentricity, a "doing your own thing," without finding that many of our needs are frustrated, and such frustration produces hostility. Some households take on the appearance of a battlefield or a wolf pack with each wolf fighting for the largest piece of meat.

3. *Uncertainty*. It's hard to follow the directions of the group with any certainty if the directions keep changing. Fads in child rearing change faster than fads in teen-age dress. Montessori one day, Summerhill the next, then Ginott the following week. "We've tried everything!" has become the mass cry of despair of today's parent.

4. *Acceptance of failure*. If the children of the others are selfish, demanding, mean little brats, it is to be expected that in following the group we will come to view such behavior as "normal" for all children. Haven't most

parents come to accept the idea that *all* teen-agers will
be sullen, rebellious, and unmanageable?

5. *Parenthood becomes a burden.* Follow the tribal
mores and there won't be much fun found in parenthood.
Though they may never admit it, we feel sure the majority of parents find the responsibilities of parenthood one
pain in the neck after another. Their children may behave
about as well as most anyone else's but such behavior is
enough to keep Mother on tranquilizers and make Daddy
long for the peace of the office.

The price of conformity is far too great and the rewards
far too skimpy. Parenthood need never be one crisis to
the next, one battle after another, one long way of the
cross up till the time the youngest marries at an early age
to escape the continuous bickering. It can be a lot of fun.
The fact that so few parents find much fun in it is only a
sad commentary on what so many have come to accept
as normal and inevitable.

Becoming a responsible parent and raising responsible
children inevitably puts one at odds with the society and
its structures, clichés and institutions, and they can be
expected to react. They may, at times, become downright
hostile. More than a few of our "child-oriented" institutions have been raised to sacred cow status. PTA, Boy
Scouts, church youth groups, and kindly kindergarten
teachers are "untouchables," about on a par with Mother's
Day, Boys Town, and Albert Schweitzer. Question any,
and you've defamed the temple. But question we must if
we are to raise our children by reason rather than rote.

If parenthood is for grownups, childhood is for learning to be grownup. More than merely a physical growth
process or a series of "stages," maturation is a learning
process. As he grows, the child learns a very large number
of facts. Two plus two equals four. The boiling point of
water is $212°F$. The femur is the longest bone in the body.
He also learns relationships. A is greater than B; B is
greater than C; therefore A is greater than C. Dark
clouds and lightning are followed by rain. There is an ob-

served relationship between dark clouds and showers. And he learns the means to attain his goals. Some means may be very effective, while some may not work too well. Some may be adaptive and others maladaptive. Some may be effective one time but not another or at one period of life but not at another. The four-year-old may find that a temper tantrum will get him what he wants. If, however, he is still pulling temper tantrums to get what he wants at sixteen, he may find not only that they are ineffective but that they are self-destructive.

As he grows up, he acquires increasingly complex goals. In the early years, his goals are what we call "primary" rewards. They are the satisfactions of basic needs: food and drink, sleep, physical comfort, and these other "basics" we think of when we think of making the young child happy. He later learns to work for "secondary" rewards: praise, recognition, acceptance, and achievement. He learns to work toward the attainment of rewards which are not immediate. This, in fact, is one of the more noticeable changes which takes place as the individual matures. It even has much to do with what we mean when we speak of maturity, and for this reason we will return to it repeatedly throughout the book. The very young child has almost no ability to tolerate a delay in his rewards.

He learns these secondary goals from others, from teachers, friends, and television, but most of all from his parents. From them he learns what is "important" and "desirable." They reward him with their praise when he strives to attain those goals which are important to them, hence their goals become his goals. Difficulties arise, however, when 1) he develops two or more goals of about equal strength which are incompatible; 2) he does not learn effective means of attaining his goals; 3) he lacks motivation for the attainment of his goals; 4) his goals, or the means he employs for their attainment, are contrary to the goals, rights, or comfort of the other members of the family.

The goals and the plans for achieving them must take into consideration all other goals so as to avoid conflicting goals. And they must take into consideration all members of the family if the individual members, both parents and children, are to avoid running roughshod over others. This is where the parents come in. As the mother and father, you are in the best position to become the "child expert" with your own children. You have a far better opportunity than anyone else to know each individual in the family, far better than a teacher, grandparent, pediatrician, or next-door neighbor. Even better than the child knows himself.

We have called our approach a *non-psychology of child rearing*. This, we admit, is misleading. We have not turned against the empirical evidence of psychology. Quite the opposite. We believe the fundamental principles derived from empirical psychology provide the guidelines for sane child rearing. On the other hand, we feel psychology has been given a bad name. So much utter nonsense has been written and spoken during the last forty years in the name of psychology, most parents have become convinced that psychologists are bereft of anything resembling common sense, and that psychology is less a science than palmistry.

In the name of psychology, the child experts have been busy selling parents programs designed to lead only to bankruptcy—physically, morally, and intellectually. For the parents as well as the children.

In a recent, well-designed study conducted at the University of California at Berkeley, the home environments of a large sample of adolescents were studied. Where the homes were easygoing, permissive, with few demands made, and little responsibility expected, trouble, by way of rebellion and delinquency, often followed. These were the homes in which the members (including the parents) pretty well "did their own thing." The parents took pride in considering themselves "modern" and "liberal." The parental roles were weak, often undefinable. A second set of homes was described as "authoritarian." The homes might also have been called "autocratic." The children were ordered about by a martinet parent (usually the father) like so many recruits in the Marine Corps. Their opinions counted for nothing. They felt they were tolerated by their parents so long as they kept their mouths shut and did as they were told. Nothing else. They also tended to rebel in hatred toward parents (and, generalizing, toward society). And they suffered both the confusion of those from the permissive homes as well as the rejection.

A third group of families was described as "authoritative." *Authoritative* families differed greatly from either *permissive* or *authoritarian*. In the authoritative families, the parents assumed their roles as parents, in both responsibility and authority. They did not permit the social anarchy of the permissive home, nor did they impose the iron-fisted tyranny of the authoritarian home. The authoritative parents recognized their children as human beings. But they did not ignore the fact they were children. The authoritative family had a structure in which all members of the family had responsibilities as well as rights. Authority remained with the parents. But it was not the authority of a dictator serving the desires of the dictator (as in the authoritarian home); it was the authority which flowed logically from the responsibility assumed by parents who cared deeply for their children, parents who enjoyed their children and wanted very much to see them grow into the full potential of their adulthood.

It might be easier if it were not so, but the fact is painfully clear: The parents who work to establish a rational authoritative home today are going to find themselves fighting a world gone mad. They will not be able to find support from other concerned parents, from their children's teachers, or from the self-styled experts. The majority are all too willing to turn the reins over to the demands of the children. And the children walk away from them in contempt. Few parents are willing to pay the price. And we do not say the price of accepting fully the mantle of parenthood is cheap.

Parenthood, we have found, is a little like family banking. We can borrow on time, mortgage what we have, live for today, and shut our eyes to that inevitable day when the bills come due. Or we can make deposits, invest for the future, and look forward to the day when we can retire in comfort and satisfaction. The investments in our children we make today will pay off for them many years from now (as well as during their childhood). It will also pay off for their father and mother. We freely admit (and we admit it to our children as well) we have no desire to spend the rest of our lives raising our children. We don't want to bail a twenty-five-year-old son out of trouble or worry over the troubled life of a thirty-year-old daughter. If we do our job responsibly now, we won't have to. Their father and mother have a life of their own. Once they are grown, we expect to live it without further concern for what we did "wrong," without the regrets we hear expressed by so many parents today.

Teachers, child experts, and some parents have accused us of advocating "only common sense." To a degree, we plead guilty. But common sense, in an area which has been so dominated by psychological nonsense, is far from common.

We feel it is high time parenthood is returned to parents. We hope you agree.

2

WHAT OUR CHILDREN
NEED FROM US

We take it for granted our children need parents, or at least someone filling the role of parent. We don't ask why, yet perhaps we should. They surely need us for something beyond board, room and clothing, but only if we can determine what our children need and why they need it, can we set realistic goals toward providing it.

A child's needs grow out of his vulnerability. If our children were self-sufficient, they wouldn't need us at all. And when they reach the age at which they should be self-sufficient, they hopefully will no longer feel any dependency, material or emotional, on their parents. Our job in the meantime is to provide for those needs while we bring our children toward self-sufficiency. If we fail to provide for their needs, the growth toward independence will be seriously impeded or arrested.

The child is born into a world he cannot understand, a world in which he cannot survive without a great deal of support and protection. For a long period of time, he will look to his parents for everything—food, drink, warmth, diaper changes, burping—*everything*. But most of these needs, as we all know, could be supplied by a household and nursing staff. And there is more to parenthood than that. Or should be. Parents provide preparation for adulthood. For the first quarter of the child's life, the father and mother provide the environment and many of the experiences from which he will learn most of what he will need in order to live a satisfying, productive, life.

Omniscience. In early childhood, the child needs to believe his parents can answer all his questions, that they can make sense out of the world so bewildering to him, that they are, in effect, omniscient. As he matures, his need for the all-knowing parent diminishes, but only gradually. Not until adolescence does he begin to understand that his parents are not authorities on everything. Even in his teens, however, he looks to them for answers and understanding of the world. Knowing that they have the answers contributes greatly to his security.

The need for omniscience in the parent is not simply a need for answers to his countless "whys." He needs to know that the most significant adults in his life have found answers for their own lives, that they can make sense out of *their* world. Answers to the whys is, nevertheless, an important part of it.

Ten-year-old Tommy's mother and father stress self-reliance. To most of his questions seeking answers ("Why does the moon sometimes look bigger?" "How does the baby get out of the mother's stomach?"), he is told to "look it up yourself." Other times, he is given a "non-answer." A non-answer is a response which does not convey information responsive to the question. The child's answer "Just 'cause" is such an answer. Tommy's parents have a long list of non-answers: "Because that's the way things are." "God wants it that way." "You'll understand when you are older." "Grownups sometimes do these things." Tommy asked his father, "What makes the light in a light bulb?" His father told him, "You turn on the switch." "Why give a long drawn-out answer," he told us, "he won't understand it." Perhaps not, but if the non-answers continue, he will soon stop asking any questions.

Tommy will probably also stop trying to make sense out of the world in which he lives. He was nearly late for school one morning when he couldn't remember where he left his homework. His father shouted at him and called him an imbecile. That evening when his parents were dressing for a dinner party, his father exploded when he couldn't recall where he left his cuff links. He blamed his wife.

When Tommy was in third grade, he was chosen to play the lead in the Christmas play. The day of the play, he was too upset to eat breakfast. His mother called him a "baby" and a "scaredy cat." She worried that he might freeze up and embarrass her before the other mothers. She sent Tommy upstairs for her bottle of tranquilizers, then sent Tommy off to school to cope with his anxiety.

The boy's father has ulcers. Tommy has heard a lot about the ulcers. Whenever he acts up, runs through the house or plays the radio or TV loudly, his mother reprimands him with "You're going to cause your father's ulcers to flare up." But once or twice each week, Tommy listens to his mother shout and scream at his father—usually over the father's drinking and straying from his ulcer diet.

If Tommy continues to look to his parents for answers for his life based upon any answers they might have found for their lives, he will be in trouble. But he won't. It won't be long before he gives up trying to make sense out of a world in which things seem so contradictory and obviously crazy.

There are, admittedly, problems for the parents in this expected role of omniscience. Alas, none of us are omniscient. Any parent who has tried to tackle new math can attest to that. We often feel unprepared to answer children's questions. As one mother told us: "I have only a high school education and my husband only completed the ninth grade." She has our sympathy. She is not alone. But it isn't a matter of number of years of schooling. One could have five Ph.D.s and still not feel at all adequate to answer all the questions a six-year-old can come up with. And it would be a full-time job for any parent to keep up with all the rapidly changing areas of learning to which our children are exposed. Thank heaven, we don't have to. Our children's need for omniscient parents does not demand we make ourselves walking authorities

on everything. What our children need to know is that
we are *willing* to answer their questions fully to the extent
of our knowledge and willing to help them find any answers we cannot provide. An encyclopedia, a yearly factual almanac, and a public library card will provide a
broad resource base.

Responsibility. By the time they reach adulthood,
our children will, hopefully, have formulated goals. Many
of these goals will be long-range. In order to reach them,
they will have to learn responsibility. They will live in a
social world in which they will have rights and obligations
in their relationships with others. They will make commitments to spouse, children, employer, and associates.
These commitments will give rise to a number of responsibilities, and the assumption of these responsibilities will
be both the test of their maturity and the measure of their
ultimate happiness. The family environment provides the
training ground in which they learn the discipline and rewards of interpersonal responsibility. Children need, most
of all, the example of responsibility they see in a father
and mother who function on a rational, concerned level
with one another and toward their children. No one has
to be told that irresponsible parents who behave in egocentric immature ways cannot, by their words alone, teach
responsibility to their children. Beyond example, children
need to be taught responsible actions toward the other
family members, their brothers and sisters as well as their
parents. They learn their responsibilities by being in-
structed in them and by the parents seeing to it the responsibilities are assumed.

Coping. Even in early childhood, the child encoun-
ters frustrations. At first, all he can do is lash out in fury:
cry, scream and kick. He needs his parents' example and
teaching if he is to learn to cope with the countless frustrations, large and small, he will run up against during
his lifetime. He needs to be taught alternative actions. He

needs parental instruction in the means of finding logical solutions to his problems. Often, he will need his parents to show him the optional choices he may make which will be more satisfying. As he grows, he will need his parents to encourage him to find his own alternatives. And he will need their example to learn the patience necessary to do so.

Strength.   The ability to cope with one's problems is often a measure of the individual's strength and courage in facing up to them. Before we can cope with a problem, we must be willing to stand our ground and confront it without copouts, without running away. The child needs to be able to rely on his parents' strength. In his early years, he is sure his mother and father are omnipotent; they can do *anything*. His dad is not only smarter than anyone else's dad, he is bigger and stronger. The strength and courage of the parents, especially the father, protect him from what can seem to be a frightening world. As he grows up, another kind of strength becomes even more important: He needs to believe on the evidence before him that his parents are strong enough to assume *their* responsibilities, without complaint, and with eagerness and optimism.

Our children need to find in us a strength of convictions, a set of firm values and ethics they see us live by. If they find vacillation, compromise, and hypocrisy in our actions, they will have difficulty building the strength necessary to maintain their own convictions as they mature. More than that, they will be learning a depressing lesson: The pressures and temptations of this world are simply too much to resist. If we don't stand up to them, how can we expect our children to believe they can?

Keith and Karen, eleven-year-old twins, have listened to their parents argue for hours over their father's habit of stopping off for a drink on the way home from work. Always, their father's excuse, "All the guys were going; I didn't feel I could be the only 'party-pooper.'" And their mother's retort: "Don't you have the guts to say no?" Apparently he doesn't or he would. But what about his wife? When a cousin from out of town arrived recently, she invited the woman over for a Sunday afternoon and evening despite the fact that she didn't like the relative, a gossipy and officious female. "I really hated to tell the twins we couldn't go on the picnic we promised, but I didn't see how I could be rude to my cousin." How much do either of the parents have the strength to withstand social pressures? The expected irony comes whenever the twins offer the excuse, "But all the other kids were doing it." Both parents jump to answer, "You have a mind of your own; you don't have to do something just because others expect it of you."

Our children also need our strength to defend them against the injustice of outsiders. This doesn't mean they need us to fight their battles when they are perfectly capable of doing so (even if they might lose), but some battles they cannot fight.

Irene is an eighth grader. She has a social studies teacher who has selected Irene to be the virtual scapegoat of the class. Although Irene has maintained a C+ average and has been no problem in behavior, the woman apparently resents the girl's tall, almost classic beauty. Last year, Irene was chosen to model for a teen fashion magazine and she has appeared in a soft drink commercial widely seen on television. On numerous occasions, the teacher has referred to Irene as "the big TV star" and "Little Miss Clothes Horse." Most recently, the woman remarked in class about "those starlets in the movies and television who get work by 'playing along' with producers and directors." When her classmates laughed and turned in her direction, Irene burst into tears and ran from the room. The teacher has now reported her to the office for leaving without permission.

Irene has little chance of fighting this injustice on her own. It is the teacher against the child, with all the power in the hands of the teacher. Irene needs the strength of her parents to counter such viciousness, parents who are concerned enough and courageous enough to take the matter to the administrators and demand something be done.

This is not to suggest parents take a "my child, right or wrong" approach. The child does need our protection, however, when he is treated unjustly by those he has been taught to obey (if not respect). This may include teachers, neighbors, relatives, and older siblings. Often we see parents who extend the protection where it is not needed: against the other parent. Mothers step in to protect their children against the supposed unfairness of fathers. Fathers side with children against their mothers. This "protection" usually does more harm than good. Our children need parents who will stand together, sometimes against the world. They decidedly do not need parents who engage in rivalry and infighting, even when it is in the name of "protecting" them.

Which brings us to what our children most need from us:

Security. This means many things in the world of a child. Everything we have described in the authoritative family is designed to contribute to his overall security, his feelings of sureness and stability.

When we speak of providing security for the child, none of us think primarily in terms of financial security. We have seen many families in Latin America living in conditions we would consider appalling poverty, yet with children who showed a security and tranquillity which would be the envy of many parents in our affluent society.

Finances are given such importance in so many homes, the child's security is bound to be affected, not so much perhaps by a lack of money (which is always relative), as by attitudes toward money and financial security.

Barbara is a frail, somewhat timid, thirteen-year-old. She has done consistently poor work in school. Psychological testing did not reveal an intellectual deficit, but did show a picture of a very frightened young lady, later confirmed in conversation. Among her fears is that her father, owner of an equipment rental company, is on the brink of financial ruin. From earliest childhood she has listened to both parents talk endlessly of each and every financial reversal—real or potential. Barbara's mother believes a child "should be made aware of reality." This, she feels, should include open discussion of financial worries. "Why shield her?" she asked. "Shouldn't she be made to face facts?" The girl's father feels such "facts of life" keep down the child's "tendency to always ask for the moon."

Of course we want our children to learn the value of money. No parent will intentionally raise a child to believe that money grows on trees. But how money values are taught can become very important. Take, for example, another extreme:

Dennis is a long-haired senior in high school, vice-president of the student body. He has applied to enter a private university on the West Coast. The tuition will run over $2000 a year, with room and board at least an equal amount. His father is deeply in debt. He suffered substantial losses on the stock market and his real estate brokerage has slumped during the past couple of years. Dennis knows nothing of this. His mother has done her best to see to that. She has opposed her husband's suggestion that Dennis be made aware of their situation and perhaps enroll in a community college near home. "The finances are our concern," she has argued. "Why should Dennis have to pay the price for our bad luck?" Her son, however, is a perceptive young man. He is unaware of the family financial picture, but he has noticed changes and he has drawn conclusions. "My mother is a real martyr case," he told us. "She never buys anything for herself, and my old man makes enough money that she could if she wanted to."

Barbara's parents are creating a world of fear for their daughter. Dennis is living in an unreal environment which will breed resentment in him when the time comes, as it will, when he discovers how little his parents have trusted his maturity and understanding.

Between the two extremes there is an answer. The child needs to be made aware of certain realities. But how much, how soon? How much information the child *needs* to know concerning the family finances can provide us with a rough guideline as to how much we share with him. In most situations, this is minimal, especially during his earlier years. He is not supporting the family and is powerless to do much about the finances one way or the other, so there is no reason to ask him to assume our anxieties. This is not to say we never tell our children, "That's too expensive" or "We cannot afford that." Teaching the children material values and what money is worth is important to their education and preparation for adulthood. The values, however, are relative, not absolute. The question "Is $500 too expensive?" is meaningless unless we specify what we are contemplating and how important, relatively, it is to us. What we want to teach our children, and what they need to learn from us is that item *A* which sells for 89 cents is too expensive (in terms of value received, practicality, etc.) while item *B* which is priced at $2.49 is a bargain. We want them to learn that when we say, "We cannot afford item *C*," we usually mean, "We cannot afford to purchase item *C* if we are going to buy items *D*, *E* and *F* which we want more." Our children can be taught money values without being traumatized. And they can be given a feeling of material security without being sheltered from all financial realities.

Occasionally, parents are concerned over the possible effects on the children's security of relocating the family when the father is transferred or accepts a new job. They may have heard that leaving the "security" of the previous home and friends will adversely affect them. They may also have heard that children need the security of close relatives (who provide "roots" and "ties"), grandparents, aunts, uncles, etc. There actually seems to be little evidence for either of these having any significant effect on the emotional security of the child—*if* the child is being raised with the stability and emotional security provided by responsible—and *loving*—parents.

Self-image. Father and Mother provide the child's affirmation of his identity as a person, a human being of special value.

More than all else, and affecting all our child will become, we want our children to grow to adulthood with substantial self-esteem. We teach them their self-image. They *need* this affirmation from us. If the child grows up in an environment of rationality and responsibility in which he, and each other member of the family, is *valued,* he will develop a positive self-image: He will learn to like himself. We use the word *valued* rather than the word *loved* since, while valuing the child is one very important way in which we love him, loving him encompasses much more. To value a child is to recognize *him,* his personality, his uniqueness, and his potential. It is to communicate to him the satisfaction and joy we find in *him,* the individual, apart from mere satisfaction with his behavior at a particular time. To *value* him is to enjoy him, his opinions, interests, and activities.

As parents, we want to like our children, and we do. Sure, they are at times annoying, but if we are assuming our responsibility in creating a wholesome family environment and raising them in a rational, mature fashion, they are generally delightful people to know. There are times, however, when we may do things to and for our children which do not communicate to them that we value them. We often act in the name of "loving" when we do so.

Bill is a nineteen-year-old college sophomore and a loner. An average student, he is one who is distinguished only by a total lack of distinction. He has dated only half a dozen times, only twice since entering college. He has never had any close friends. As he puts it, "I don't have much of a personality and I guess I must turn people off, so what's the point in trying to make friends?" Recently, he decided to drop out of college at the end of the current semester. "No, I don't have any plans. I suppose I'll just enlist in the vast army of losers."

Bill had a protective mother who divorced Bill's father when the boy was four. Most of their conflicts centered on differences over the raising of their only child. At five, she would not allow Bill to play with other children his age on the block. "They were all such rough children," she explained, "even the little girls." At ten, Bill wanted a bike. "I was the only kid for blocks who didn't have one," he said. His mother would not hear of it, even though his grandparents offered to buy one for him for Christmas. "Just the very thought of him riding a bicycle sends chills down my spine," she told the grandparents; "kids get killed on them every day." She had similar feelings when she turned down his pleas to be permitted to get a driver's license. (Bill has started to drive only within the past year.) She was always very concerned for his health. Each time he came down with a mild cold (which was frequent), he was taken to the doctor "just to be on the safe side." Despite all the restrictions she placed on his activities and the disappointments he felt throughout his childhood due to them, Bill is somehow sure he was loved by his mother "more than the average kid." "If she hadn't loved me so much, she wouldn't have been so concerned."

Loving, however, is only loving if it meets the needs of the one "loved." And perhaps the most important *need* of the child is the need to be seen as worthwhile. Bill is pathetically lacking in self-esteem. And understandably so. With her overprotection, his mother communicated: "You are inadequate." The child's mind leaps to the inference: "If my parents won't let me ride a bike (or go on a hike, or own an air rifle, or etc.) it must be because they don't believe I am as capable as other kids my age."

"You're no good" can be communicated in other ways

as well. "Spoiling" the child is one. The so-called child experts and those parents following them who advocate a permissive "let the kids do their own thing" philosophy cannot hold a genuine love for children—any children. A colleague of ours once expressed it very well when she said, "You have to hate a child to spoil it." Spoiling a child is a way of saying, "I don't care enough to say no."

Eleven-year-old Audrey is being robbed of her self-esteem in another, tragically common way. Her parents have a rocky marriage. While their relationship is, by outward appearances, no worse than many of their friends, and they have never seriously contemplated divorce, they have engaged in a struggle over nearly everything. His job, her friends, finances, sex, his parents, household chores, and child rearing are all running issues which keep the household in continual turmoil. Both parents displace their hostility. Audrey gets the brunt of their anger. She has become convinced she can do nothing right and everything wrong. She is hollered at for every little thing. What has eroded the girl's self-esteem, however, is the obviously pernicious relationship between her parents. Audrey is an only child. She sees her parents are unhappy with each other, and rightly or wrongly she feels they are staying together because of her. Her conclusion: "I am the cause of my parents' unhappiness. I must be a bad person to do this to them."

Her parents have never tried to give her this impression. They haven't felt they were staying together for her sake. But the mind of a child easily builds conclusions on subjective feelings. As adults, we have learned that our actions do not cause and determine all events in the world about us. We had a childhood in which to learn it. The perceptions of the young child are almost totally egocentric. We recall talking to a young woman whose father had served with the U. S. Army in Europe during World War II. In the spring of 1945 she was in the second grade. One day she told her mother she wanted to write a letter to the President of the United States asking him to end the war and bring her daddy home. Her mother helped her write the letter and she sent it off to the White House. Shortly after, the war in Europe came to an end and her father, wounded in the closing days, was flown home. It took a long time, she told us, before she could accept the fact that it was not her letter which had brought it all about. In the egocentric, and very normal, magical thinking of a child, all events are in some way brought about by his wishes or actions. The child wanted her father home, so she stopped the war. In similar fashion, if the child's parents are unhappy with each other, the child suffers guilt for what he assumes he has caused.

One further example of "teaching" a negative self-image: The child will lack self-esteem if the parents do not *realistically* praise his achievements. The key word is italicized. If he is criticized for virtually everything, he may decide he can't win and he will stop trying. If the parents, on the other hand, in an effort to give encouragement, praise too much, it may have an equally bad effect. Lavish praise, when it is unmerited, not only loses its value as a reward and motivator, it is disparaging.

If the child is praised almost equally for doing a mediocre job and doing an excellent job, why should we expect the extra effort? Self-esteem may be lost when and if he concludes that the praise he gets from his parents for the job poorly done means they don't believe he is capable of anything better. The schools are more guilty of praising without merit than most parents, but many parents, influenced by teachers and the *don't-permit-failure* child psychologists, fall into the same error.

Our children need our praise for their achievement, but only when it is a valid recognition of achievement commensurate with their potential.

Limits. Imagine you have taken a new job and you show up the first day unaware of the nature of your duties. You report to the boss; he greets you cordially, shows you around, and introduces you to your co-workers. They

are engaged in a variety of activities. The boss shows you
to your new office and tells you your secretary will be able
to requisition anything you may need. You ask him
about your duties. He shrugs. "That's up to you; you may
discover something you'll find interesting." You ask about
hours, days off, and vacation. His answer is the same to
each question: "Suit yourself." Let's say this went on for
two or three weeks. No assignments. No direction. Always
the same answer: "Suit yourself." The frustration could
become maddening. We all want structure in our lives.
We want to know the name of the game and the rules,
the demands and expectancies. Children, even more than
adults, need structure in their lives. They are even less
certain of the outcome of their actions if left to themselves.
A magazine cartoon pictured a small boy in a progressive
kindergarten asking his teacher, "Do we really have to
do what we want to do?" The fact is, none of us want to
have to do what we want to do if it means acting with no
direction. The mature adult is able to pursue long-range
goals under *self*-direction, but there *is* direction. The child
is limited in this ability. He cannot give himself direction when he is unaware of the choices available and
the consequences which will follow. The awareness
comes from experience. The child both needs and *wants*
direction and limits. When his parents are involved enough
to set limits on his behavior and see to it that he keeps
within the limits, it assures him he is *safe* in the world:
They wouldn't let him do anything which might be harmful to him.

We recall a sixteen-year-old boy we were asked to test.
He was in juvenile detention waiting trial for murder. He
had a record of trouble, mostly minor offenses, since he
was eight. Each time, his parents bailed him out of the
difficulty. His father was a business executive and several
times the family had moved across country. Three or four
times the transfer came up at a time when the boy had
run into trouble with the authorities. Each time he was re-

leased to his parents when it was explained to the court they were leaving the area. At no time had he been confined for more than a few hours, nor was he ever given any psychiatric help. As the district attorney said, "Everybody played musical chairs with this kid; and he just happened to be in my jurisdiction when the music stopped." The boy's story came out in bitterness that bordered on rage. "I used to wish sometimes my folks would ground me or chew me out or, well hell, anything! Do you know something? Never, not even once, did my old man tell me I *couldn't* do something. He let me get away with murder! That's really funny, isn't it? The joke's on him 'cause it looks like I can't get away with this one."

Limits for the child are somewhat like the boundaries that mark our property. If we don't know the boundaries of our front yard, we cannot risk putting in any improvements. We might be trespassing and find, after the brick wall is built or the shade tree is planted, the improvements we paid for are on our neighbor's land and must be removed. Knowing the boundaries provides security. We can move freely within them. Providing the security of limits to the child is one very important way in which we express our love for him. He needs parents with the concern and courage to say "No."

Role Identity.   At birth, infant boys are tagged with blue identification bracelets, and girls with pink. The sex role learning begins. From then on, he and she will be taught to act, react, think, talk, and feel as male or female, that is, what our society says is male or female. Despite those who talk of wanting "to be a person first and a man or woman second," the fact remains: There is no neuter gender. We are born male or female. In time, we become a man or woman. *Man* and *woman* are learned roles. They become identities.

We could appropriately discuss role identities under education. It is a part of the child's education, a most crucial part. Yet because it so often goes on without conscious teaching on the part of parents and the other adults in the child's life, we tend to overlook the teaching role we play in the child's development of a sexual identity.

Even if we give it little thought and less planning, we do teach our sons who and what they are expected to be as boys, later men, and our daughters what they are to be as girls, later women.

Children are today being presented with an almost hopelessly confusing sex role identity. The goal of unisex may not be far off, and in much more than dress and hair length. The past two decades have seen major break-downs in sexual distinctions, and each time a sex role distinction has crumbled, it has been applauded by the avant-garde as a step toward equality. Women's Liberation sees the dawning of a new day in which child rearing will be a joint responsibility shared by Father, Mother, and government-supported child-care centers with no role distinctions.

Utopia? Closer to emotional chaos! The more we have moved in this direction, the more we have turned out children who are confused, frustrated, and hostile. We have also produced a society of mothers who bitterly resent the responsibilities of motherhood and fathers who are little more than breadwinners and figureheads.

A few decades ago, nobody had to tell a child how Daddy differed from Momma in their roles. He was aware of more than just "Daddy goes to an office and brings home money." He knew what his father did to earn a living. He often saw him doing it. He knew what Mother did; he watched her every day. Of one thing he was sure: Men did one thing; women, another. Fathers were fathers. Mothers were mothers.

Not today. A six-year-old girl told us, "My father teaches at my school. My mother is a judge. There is this long-haired boy who baby-sits me. I guess he's a hippy. I don't know what I'll be when I grow up." Perhaps very con-fused!

A significant shift came when the father moved from the farm or blacksmith shop or corner grocery to the corporate office or plant. In countless suburban homes, Father leaves for work before the children are off to school. He may commute many miles and return shortly before the children go to bed. His job may require him to fly to distant cities and be away for days at a time. He is simply not physically present in the home. Hence, the authority and influence fall to the mother. He is the silent and absent member of the family.

The father working at a desk in a complex corporation may have a difficult time convincing his children he is productively working. Children believe what they can see. They see Mother bake the cookies they eat and iron the clothes they wear. They don't see what Daddy does at the office. If, in addition, he plays little part in the family during what little time he is at home, he provides no sex role model: Just what is a man and a father?

The mother's role today may be no less vague. The majority of mothers are holding outside jobs and many who stay home are unhappy with their lot. Most mothers find they are thinly stretched between PTA meetings, shopping trips, transporting children, husband, and housework. Little wonder so many face an identity crisis. Their answers to "Who and what am I?" could fill several pages.

There are no simplistic answers to the problems created by the pressures on both husband and wife. And there are no longer stereotypic roles for men and women. Fortunately, they are assigned to the past. Teaching boys that "all girls are . . ." and teaching girls that certain activities are "only for boys" is one major reason so many husbands and wives relate so poorly. We don't want to teach these distinctions and discriminations to our children. The roles of Father and Mother can also no longer be shoved into stereotypic cubbyholes. There are no roles which are established as befitting the *nature* of a man or woman. Roles are learned.

The child learns his sexual role through emulation and identification. He or she imitates the model presented by the parent. Or if he finds the model unacceptable, he seeks his identity elsewhere.

Children worship heroes and look for heroes to worship. The heroes, whether or not in reality, seem to embody the virtues and attributes the child finds appealing. The *omniscience* and *omnipotence* the child looks for in his parents are a part of this hero worship. If the father is *present*, emotionally as well as physically, he fills a parental role equal in responsibility to, but distinct from, that of his wife and, furthermore, if he shows evident satisfaction in his life, his sons will seek to emulate him and identify with him. And his daughters will find in him a positive model of manhood. If the girls see a mother who fully enjoys being a woman and who obviously finds joy in loving their father, they will grow up with a pride in their sex which will contribute greatly to a healthy self-image.

Phillip is a senior in high school, the eldest of three. This year he has been involved in a student activist movement seeking to abolish the school dress code, establish an open campus and a policy barring all "pigs" from campus. He and his friends have had several heated confrontations with the school vice-principal. They have broken several windows in the administration offices and have threatened to burn the school if their demands are not met.

Phillip's father manages a chain department store, a position he has held, and hated, for fourteen years. He dropped out of law school when Phillip was born and money ran out. Phillip has seldom heard his father refer to the job as anything other than "the salt mines." The boy has also listened to his father express bitterness toward his wife and cynicism toward marriage (which he calls "the mutual bear trap").

Phillip has no interest in following in his father's footsteps. The father has talked long and hard of the value of a good education, hard work, and "making something of yourself." Phil wants no part of any of it. "Who wants to end up like him?" he asks. He is in open rebellion against his father and everything his father stands for.

In earlier years, Phillip identified more with his mother. He was closer to her in every way. Even when he was home, which was usually no more than three evenings a week, Phillip's father almost never entered into the role of parent. When the children had questions or problems, they went to their mother. (By the time they entered high school, they didn't go to either parent.) What discipline there was, and there wasn't much, the mother handled. Finally, Phillip rebelled against his mother's indulgent momism as strongly as he rebelled against his father's indifference.

Something very similar happens to many girls. In discussing their future with a group of about ninety high school girls, we found only three who felt there was something attractive and desirable in the role of housewife, and only nine who did not feel that men have the major advantages in life. While about a third of the girls believed their mothers were "reasonably satisfied" with their role of housewife, the majority of these girls felt the satisfaction stemmed, rather ironically, from an inability to do much of anything else.

Unless a girl finds it desirable to be female, she will always, without exception, develop negative feelings toward herself. She is born female. She cannot change that simple biological fact. If she finds nothing good in being female, she won't find much good in herself.

The specific roles assumed by the mother and father are not too important. Circumstances will vary. Mothers may work, fathers may clean house. Mothers may play baseball with their sons, fathers may teach the children to cook. What is important is that the child is able to recognize that both Father and Mother assume responsibilities and authority, and that both are very much involved in their roles as spouses and parents. Even more important is that our children are able to see a father who is confident in his manhood, capable, self-assured, and fulfilled; and a mother who finds similar satisfactions in her womanhood. It is in filling these roles that the parents meet the child's need for a sexual identity.

3

WHAT THEY DON'T NEED

Of the roles our children need us to play, all can best be played by never losing sight of the fact that *we are their parents*. That word "parent" means a lot of things and includes many responsibilities. If we expand the role to include many of the subroles currently popular with some parents, however, we may provide our children with what they definitely do *not* need from us, what could, in fact, work against what we hope to give them. These are some of the things they do not need from their parents:

A Playmate. He doesn't need his father or mother to be a *pal*. He can meet playmates at school and in his neighborhood. He doesn't need to find two more playmates in his parents.

Being a playmate to your children is a role which has been popularized in the past three decades, mostly among the middle classes and upper middle classes. Before, the social worlds of adults and children were kept "worlds apart." The grownups talked among themselves; the children went off to play—with other children. Parents did not, except on rare occasions, *play* with their children.

Perhaps it started with urbanization. The increased leisure time available when the family left the farm for the city and the parents were no longer working from dawn till dark with older children working in the fields beside them called for new roles. Whatever the origin, parents were now told they *must* play with their children—under pain of guilt feelings for having rejected their offspring.

Women's magazines and periodicals for parents have had a field day pushing the parent-playmate role. Reams of copy has rolled off the presses, articles telling how to plan a fun time indoors on a rainy day (with the good mother dropping everything to invent games to play with her young ones), pieces advising fathers how to play baseball with their sons, and advertisements for mother-daughter sports outfits ("Which one is the daughter?"). Then, of course, there have been the ever-present child "experts" who have added Thou Shalt Play with Your Child to the commandments of child rearing.

What's wrong with playing with your children? Answer: Nothing—necessarily. However, a child *needs* a parent. He does not need the parent as a playmate. If, as we sometimes see, the parent is attempting to cling to his or her own childhood by "entering the play world of the child," the child may lose a much needed parent. Parents can play with their children if both parents and children enjoy doing so and most parents find fun in it, but it should not be done as an obligation, and the parents do not have to stop being parents when they play.

Marion is a vivacious thirty-three-year-old mother of four. Her eldest daughter, Janice, is fifteen, the child of Marion's first marriage. Marion was pregnant during her senior year in high school and married the girl's father a week after graduation. In school, Marion had been extremely popular, a cheer leader and homecoming queen. Now, with a daughter in high school, Marion seems to be trying to turn back the clock. She has begun dressing like her daughter, wearing look-alikes. She urges her daughter to bring home friends and she joins them in their activities as "one of the gang." She dances the latest rock dances with the high school boys and openly flirts with teen-age boy friends of her daughter. Janice has seen through it. Several times she has exploded at her mother and told her to "act your age." Recently, she has stopped bringing friends home.

It is one thing to be friendly and hospitable to your children's friends. You want them to feel welcome. But what Marion has been doing is something very different. In becoming, or trying to become, a playmate and one of the gang, she is denying her daughter what she most needs from her: a mother.

Husbands and wives frequently find themselves at odds over this question of playing with the children.

Blanche and Carl have been married sixteen years, and for fourteen of those years, since shortly after the birth of the first of their children, Blanche has been convinced her husband "doesn't care a thing about the children." "When they were very little, he practically ignored them. He'd come home from work and bury himself in the newspaper or stand out in the kitchen talking to me. He didn't seem to be aware they were even around. The kids, of course, were eager to see him and they would run to the door when they heard him drive up, but do you suppose he would take time to play with them like any normal father would? Not on your life! I've told him I don't know how many times, 'A boy needs a father to teach him to play baseball and go fishing with him or even to just wrestle with him on the living-room floor.' But I might as well be talking to a stone wall. I can't get through to Carl. Maybe somebody else can." Blanche is right about one thing: Carl is not crazy about playing with infants, his own or anyone else's. And Carl is not alone among fathers. Many fathers become interested in talking and playing with their children only when the children are old enough to interact on a conversational level. Girls grow up playing with dolls. In their teens, most of them baby-sit. Boys, on the other hand, have no experience with dolls, and in adolescence they usually have less contact with small children. They pick up the infant and they feel they are all thumbs, and they fear dropping the little one. If they play kitchy-koo games, they feel foolish. Some fathers enjoy playing baseball with their sons; others don't. Some get a kick out of roughhousing with the kids (if their wife doesn't jump on them for being "too rough"); others find it simply exhausting. If Father and child find activities they *both* enjoy, great! But if not, play should be left alone. It should never become a parental obligation, borne grudgingly, nor a chore done at the insistence of a spouse or society. The child will know, and no child wants a martyr parent. Some years ago, a father and his young son sat in our office. "My wife says I'm not a good father," the man told us. "I don't know how she can say that. Why, I've even taken the little bastard to a baseball game every week!" After two or three outings with an attitude like that, we would bet the boy would rather skip the whole thing.

A father has something unique to offer his child: his interests and enthusiasm. He has himself to offer. It may be an interest in bird-watching, football, or great books. These he can share without the sharing becoming a "cross." And this applies as well to mothers. To engage in activities which are resented creates guilt in the child, and *that* our children most certainly don't need from us.

A Servant. Few parents set out to wait on their children. Most want their children to learn to assume responsibility. Somewhere along the way, however, something goes haywire and they end up playing the role of servants to their children. Frequently, what has happened is quite simple: The child has won a game of holding out. If Mother orders the toys picked up eleven times without compliance, she may give up and go ahead and do the job herself. If the teen-age son manages to misplace tools and spill cans of paint when given the chore of cleaning the garage, Dad may do it himself next time the garage needs cleaning. And one of the most common: If two or more children are assigned a job such as cleaning up the kitchen after dinner, and a fight ensues over who is to do which chore and who is doing more than someone else, Mother may end up sending all of them out of the kitchen and doing the job herself just to keep peace and her sanity.

Children can become skillful manipulators, and there are many ways they can manipulate their parents into waiting on them. When it happens with some consistency, the parents can begin to feel they are being "had." In time, they may think in terms of the "sacrifices" they make for their children—again, the martyr syndrome. Children are quick to pick up such resentment and the rejection it implies. Furthermore, the child needs to be taught to *do* for himself; he doesn't learn when we do for him.

"But I have to keep after him so long to get him to do what he is told." Often, it may be easier to do the job ourselves. Parents can wear themselves out repeating commands which are ignored. Is there any way to break it? Yes. To understand how, let's take an example from studies in learning theory. If we take a rat which has been trained to run through a maze to reach a pellet of food and we begin administering a painful electric shock to him *each and every time* he runs the maze, he will stop after only two or three more runs. If, on the other hand, instead of giving the shock *each* time, we administer it at *aperiodic* intervals, say the first, third, fifth, and eighth times, our rat may continue to run the maze indefinitely. We might imagine the rat saying to himself, "I might as well take my chances; I was lucky the last time; maybe I will be again." *Aperiodically reinforced (punished) responses are very resistant to extinction.* This is equally true of aperiodic reward, which explains why adults continue to feed coins into a slot machine—about the time they are ready to quit, they get a few coins back. If the child has learned from experience he will be punished not after the fourth time or the seventh or the ninth, but after the *first* infraction and after each infraction, he will probably comply and the tiring repetition can cease. Frequently, all children learn is the game of parental roulette: "Maybe I can get away with it one more time before Mom blows her top."

Another thing which helps to establish the parent as servant is the socially reinforced fear of parents that they may be "demanding too much" of the children. They look around and see how little other parents ask of their children. Then they worry. If they have any doubts about it, they can expect their children to tell them: "None of my friends has to do that." And maybe they don't. But we haven't run into many parents who are violating either the letter or spirit of the child labor laws. Even farm youngsters today know nothing of the chores which were the usual routine of rural childhood a few decades ago. The child learns a valuable lesson when he is taught that he is a *member* of the family, not a guest, and family membership carries responsibilities as well as privileges. Parents need only to be concerned with whether the tasks are assigned with justice to ensure that one child does not become the Cinderella of the family. This doesn't mean the parents have to become scrupulous in dividing up the chores, only reasonable. Children can be expected to feel picked on by being made to do more than the others. This is something parents can't escape. We can do only what we think is right and fair and let it go at that. And we can refuse to be swayed by what other parents may choose to do with their children. The message we expect our children to understand is: *Family membership demands a cooperative effort. We each owe a responsibility to the other members and this includes sharing in the work to be done —whatever may be assigned.*

A "Full-time" Parent.   Parenthood is a twenty-four-hour a day responsibility. It isn't a role which can be turned on and off or delegated to others. Children definitely need parents who are fully aware of their responsibilities, but they do not need the sort of parents who devote their lives—*totally*—to their offspring. The effect on the child of the "dedicated" mother and/or father who lives only for him can be as disastrous as child neglect.

Diane is the mother of two—Kenneth, eight, and Francine, five. She and Ken, her husband, have never had a vacation away from the children, not even overnight.

Rarely do they go out for the evening. "I just don't feel right leaving the children," Diane told us. "My mother lives some distance away, and she is the only one I would trust to baby-sit my children."

Ken's reactions are understandable. "Bitter? Damned right I'm bitter. As soon as we had kids, she stopped being my wife. Everything is the kids. Nothing else counts. I might as well be a boarder. Last year I won a trip for two to Hawaii for being top sales agent. Do you think she'd leave the kids? Hell, no! I had to turn the tickets back."

Not only are Ken and Diane paying a price for Diane's "devotion." Their children are suffering from it, and can be expected to pay an even greater price in future years. Unless they openly rebel to escape their mother's "smothering," they will develop an unhealthy degree of dependency. They also may be increasingly caught in the middle of a bitter rivalry with their father (if their father does not withdraw entirely—a not implausible possibility). Furthermore, the children are likely to develop into thoroughly egocentric human beings, expecting the service and attention of all with whom they come in contact. And one further strong probability: They will carry into adulthood a crippling indebtedness (and underlying resentment) to a mother who has "sacrificed" her life for her children.

For the children's sake as well as their own, husband and wife need to retain a life of their own. Dates, late suppers for two, weekends, and vacations away from children, all go hand-in-hand with that all-important lock on the master bedroom door. Children *do* need to know their parents still have a love affair going for themselves. They don't need the single-role "devoted" parent.

A Communal Parent. No child needs more than two parents. Two work out fine if both are doing their job. More than two, and the parenthood breaks down. Children do *not* need parents by consensus—a vote of neighbors, teachers, grandparents, and scoutmasters.

All parents delegate some of their authority to others who stand *in loco parentis:* baby-sitters, teachers, etc. But this is not, or should not be, a delegation of parental responsibility. Nor a sharing of parental judgment.

Today, much of the emphasis is toward raising children as a sort of communal effort. Parents rely on outsiders for advice, direction, and decisions to an extent which amounts to a shared parenthood. Little wonder children lack confidence in their parents. The parents have no confidence in themselves. Decisions should be based on parental judgment and backed by parental authority, not submitted to a neighborhood plebiscite. Even when professional help is called for, it is important that the role of the parents be maintained. In order to do so, we seldom take a child into any extensive counseling or psychotherapy. If it is at all possible, we feel it is better in every way to work with the parents and let them work to restructure the child's environment without an intervention which would establish us as "super-parents." Unfortunately, school counselors frequently do not follow similar policies.

Possessions, Things, and Junk. Parents have been bludgeoned for years by the advertising agencies. Those Saturday morning cartoon shows have sold millions of dollars worth of battery-operated, breakable, plastic junk toys. Do children need them? Of course not! They are huckstered to parents through children by the persuasion of "other-directedness" (if every other child on the block has one, must your child be the deprived outsider?), and by repetitious pleadings which wear down parents like water dripping on a stone. Parents may gripe about it, but most go along with it, even though they realize, somehow, that adding to the toy-pollution explosion is not contributing to the health, welfare, or growth of their children.

The so-called "educational" toys are no exception. They

may look like they could offer some educational value. Some even may. The value, however, is seldom worth the investment. A good example is the plastic "shoe" designed to aid in teaching the child how to lace and tie a shoe. Wouldn't it make more sense to teach him to lace and tie his own shoe? And what is wrong with using the household alarm clock to teach him to tell time rather than bringing home a plastic toy clock? The manufacturers are no fools. They know parents are concerned with their children's education. Label the toy "educational," and parents will take the bait. Few toys on the market have much real educational value. And even fewer, despite the claims, teach the child anything in the way of *creativity*. Creative play is not encouraged by structuring the play materials, yet most toys labeled "creative" are, by their very design, rigidly structured. A toy space capsule is just that, nothing more. The child would have a hard time playing with it as anything but a space capsule. Two old tires, on the other hand, or a large packing box can be a space ship, a sailboat, a fort, pirates' cave, or doll house. Play, at its best, is imaginative. It permits the child to explore and create within the world of his fantasies. Structured toys inhibit the exploration. They also limit learning. The child playing with the plastic space capsule is not discovering the world of small bugs crawling in the garden, the colors in the rocks, or the delicate veins in a leaf.

Many parents satiate their children with toys and other assorted "things." It may be done for reasons of the parents' status needs, surrender to the child's pestering or "spoiling"—giving *things* as a substitute for love. Children enjoy toys and parents enjoy giving them, but the child does not need an endless supply which contributes only to the boredom we see in so many.

Freedom from Responsibility. When we speak of the "joys of childhood," too often (though we may not admit it) we are thinking of the freedom from responsibility. We frequently present a "double message" when we speak to our children of growing up. We tell a child he must grow up. But why should he *want* to? In the very next breath we tell him to have fun while he can "because when you grow up, you'll have to knuckle down to responsibility." Responsibility is presented as a crown of thorns adults must wear. Then why become an adult?

The person who says childhood is the period of greatest joy was never a child—or suffers from a defective memory. Childhood is a painful period, liberally sprinkled with frustration, confusion, and tears. There are times of joy, hopefully, but the joy doesn't come from being *free* of responsibility, either in childhood or adulthood. The mature adult doesn't merely accept responsibility; he seeks it. And he finds satisfaction in it.

Our overall goal in child rearing is to bring our children to an adulthood which will be rewarding. It will not be, however, if adulthood is nothing but a millstone of responsibility in which they find no pleasure. And that is what will occur unless we teach them to assume increasing responsibilities during their growth years, learning, as they go along, to take pride and satisfaction in them.

Teaching the child responsibility and seeing to it that he assumes it is not a popular idea. It's almost as outmoded as self-discipline. But every bit as important. The pseudopsychologists say they are concerned that children may have excessive demands made upon them, that they may be pressured, that their expression may be stifled, and that they can learn responsibility only if they are permitted to be free in making their choices. Too bad they don't turn their brains back on! Some of the young who are being encouraged to freely express themselves and "let it all hang out" are doing so with fire bombs! No one learns to accept responsibility by being permitted to avoid it. We demand that the child assume responsibilities and he in time learns to do so—and he learns the rewards that follow.

Copouts. These are the excuses we give ourselves and others for our failures and irresponsibilities. We often fail to see them for what they are. We may think they are reasonable, valid explanations. They are, nevertheless, excuses designed to allow us to escape facing up to what we should be doing and what we are capable of doing. And we are teaching copouts to our children.

Billy is ten years old and big for his age. He sat beside his mother across the desk and blew bubble gum into his harmonica. Not the most likable child in the world. He had compiled a very poor scholastic record in fifth grade, and not much better the year before, yet his IQ was above average and he showed no signs of emotional or physical problems which might have contributed to it. His mother provided the explanation—and the copout: "It's that teacher who should be in here. No wonder Billy couldn't do well. She simply couldn't relate to him at all. She was incapable of establishing a necessary rapport with Billy." Her son couldn't have been more in agreement. "Yeah," he said, "she's a real loser, a nothin'."

When Billy reaches sixteen, he may burn the high school when he decides the classes are not "relevant." Later, he may move from job to job when he "can't stand the pressures of a large corporation." He will be able to blame woes on his wife, suburbia, neighbors, a low income, and his mother. (The latter, we admit, may not be entirely unjustified.)

There was a recent story of a lawsuit filed in San Francisco by a young woman who claimed she was so distraught by a cable car accident she became sexually promiscuous and was driven to have relations with an incredible number of men. She collected damages! And that, we submit, should win the copout of the year award.

As young Johnny and Jane progress along the way toward adulthood, we can be sure they will be given more than enough copouts by friendly teachers, friends, and maiden aunts. The parent of today has a job with a lot of overtime trying to fight off such "helpfulness" and teach self-reliance and responsibility. Yet if we don't, we can look forward with horror to a generation in which no one accepts the consequences of running a red light or screaming "Fire!" in a crowded theatre.

Copouts are always self-defeating. Children need parents who are willing to teach, by example as well as words, that we are all accountable for our own choices, that we succeed or fail on our own, that we expect something of them other than excuses—just as we do of ourselves.

4

WHAT WE WANT FOR THEM
—AND FROM THEM

It's hard for any of us to be honest about child rearing. If we are asked, "What do you want *from* your children and *for* your children?" it is not an easy task to dig deep into ourselves and extract an answer which would reflect our true feelings. We all know those answers good parents are expected to give: "I want them to be happy," "I want them to grow up well-adjusted," etc. Nothing is wrong with these answers, except they don't say much. They are vague and abstract, something like a Fourth of July political speech. We may not disagree with them. But they don't provide a nibble of food for thought. Strip away the abstractions, and what have we? Our goals (and let's not lose sight of the fact that they are *our* goals, not necessarily our children's) are much more down to earth than that. If, that is, we have formulated goals.

We want to raise our children in such a way they will:

1. *Achieve in those areas we, their parents, consider worthwhile.* Sure, we say we want our children to pursue their own interests; we don't want to impose our goals on them, but how would we react if a daughter announced she planned to become a topless dancer?

2. *Behave in accord with our values and those of our social peer group.* We may not be able to control what they think and believe, but we want to at least hear them verbalize our set of values (even though we may deny it).

3. *Conform to our standards of conduct within the family and elsewhere.*

4. Be happy in their life, well adjusted, and free of physical and emotional problems.

5. Develop the maturity as well as abilities which will permit them to face the world on their own.

But even these goals don't tell much. They are still too vague and abstract. Furthermore, they are quite obviously the *result* of many decisions and many activities day by day, what we do as parents, and what they do in response. What we are looking for, then, is a series of *responses*.

We ask our son to carry out the trash. He responds with:

1. "Why do I always have to be the one to do it?"
2. "I'm watching my favorite program; I'll do it later."
3. "Sure, Mom."
4. "Do it yourself!"

Wouldn't we all like to count on Number 3 and never have to hear the defiance of Number 4? Then Number 3 is our *goal response.*

Suzy, a twelve-year-old, is a bright girl, considerably above average intellectually. Her teacher reports:

1. She does well in her studies but is often late in completing assignments.
2. She excels in subjects which interest her, but pays little attention to subjects she dislikes.
3. She does excellent work in her studies but is quiet, withdrawn, a "loner."
4. She is an excellent student, earns top grades, is well liked by teachers, and popular with fellow students.

Number 4 would be our goal response—the sort of behavior we want from her.

Suzy's sixteen-year-old sister is out on a date with her steady boy friend. He parks in a secluded spot and begins "making out." She responds:

1. By pulling away from him and asking to be taken home.
2. By going along with kissing and embracing but will not allow him to touch her breasts or try any further petting.

3. By going along with heavy petting, stopping short of mutual stimulation to orgasm.

4. By mutual stimulation to orgasm but refusing to engage in intercourse.

5. By going all the way with sexual intercourse if her boy friend has thought to bring along a condom.

Selecting a goal response in this situation may be more difficult. Sex presents a more complex question. It is most certainly more serious in its possible ramifications than carrying out the trash. And the goal response we may want to attempt to teach will reflect our own unconscious as well as conscious attitudes, healthy and/or unhealthy. Simply arriving at our decision can call for some soul-searching. If Number 1 is our desired choice, does it mean we view *all* sex as bad, sex before marriage as bad, or the particular boy as undesirable? If we go along with Number 5, is it because we want to do the "modern thing," because we feel the kids are going to do it anyway and so long as they take precautions to avoid pregnancy, okay, or because we believe sexual experience is desirable if it will help prevent future sexual hang-ups?

First, we have to decide which of several responses is our goal. In most situations, the choice will be almost immediately apparent. In others, we will hang on the horns of a dilemma. One major stumbling block in the path of child rearing is the reluctance of many parents to confront these choices and arrive at *some* decision—*any* decision. It becomes a sort of chronic avoidance of goal setting. Uncomfortable though it may be, specific goal responses *must* be selected before the next steps may be taken. And unless we are to find ourselves continually reacting rather than acting, the goals must be selected *in advance*. Judging all responses after the fact, and punishing those we judge undesirable, is both unjust and ineffective to any learning.

Let's assume now that we have selected a goal response. To understand something of how to elicit this response, it is necessary to understand the basics of learning, how it takes place, and the role we parents play teaching our children these goal responses.

All learning involves reward and/or punishment. We learn to seek those experiences which have, in the past, proven rewarding. We learn to avoid those which have been punishing. We can use the word *pleasurable* for rewarding and *painful* for punishing. The principle works essentially the same in *all* learning, whether we are talking about learning to drive a car or learning to sing opera or learning to converse with a child. If we drive the car cautiously and correctly, we are *rewarded* by arriving at our destination safely; if we drive improperly or recklessly, we may be punished by getting a traffic ticket or wrapping our car around a pole.

Reward and/or punishment is not *one* way through which leaning occurs: It is the *only* way. We feel this is one of those empirical facts which will strike the reader as glaringly obvious. Why then has it escaped so many contemporary educational theorists who scribble endlessly about "the total pedological environment" and "learning for the sake of learning" with no attempt to identify and *employ*—the rewards and punishments essential to any learning? We read of "unmotivated" learning, learning which supposedly occurs without reinforcement, reward or punishment, but when we take a look at the examples given, we discover, sure enough, there has been some reward and/or punishment. Or the learning has not occurred. Our eldest son had been driving by himself for only a few weeks. He had gone along many times *as a passenger* when we had driven from our home to the business district of the city. He now was going downtown alone. "Dad, what's the best way to get there?" he asked. We suggested he take the route we always took, but he had to ask several more questions to be sure he knew which streets and how to get on them. With someone else driving the car, he had no *reason* to learn, no reward or punishment. And little or no learning had occurred.

A short time ago on television we listened to a self-styled child authority. As close as we can come to quoting him, he made the following statement: "The child has an innate desire to learn. If given the freedom to explore the world about him, without demands that he learn specific tasks and employ specified materials, this innate drive will lead him to educate himself." We don't say there is no truth to the statement, as far as it goes. But it stops short of being valid. Certainly, if we permit Willie the freedom to explore the hot stove, he may discover how fingers are burned. If we let him wander at will in and out of his parents' bedroom, he may learn something about sex. But children have individual interests just as adults do, and we feel sure many children could be raised in a home with an entire library of books on mathematics without ever once showing any desire, innate or otherwise, to learn multiplication tables.

It is popular (and sounds impressive) to talk of "making learning fun," "encouraging creativity," "permitting the child to explore his world." It sounds so psychologically sophisticated. But perhaps we should face facts. Learning is *not* always *fun*. It is often tedious and can be even downright painful. The medical student may be dedicated to medical science; he may look forward to a satisfying career as a physician; but at 3:00 A.M. the night before examinations when he is poring, with bloodshot eyes and countless cups of coffee, over an histology text, we doubt he would describe the learning as "fun."

Jimmy, eleven years old, hounded his parents for months for a guitar. Finally, for Christmas, they bought the guitar and arranged for lessons. Jimmy walked ten feet off the ground. He showed off the guitar to all his friends, even took it to school to show. Following his first lesson, his mother had to virtually drag him away from the guitar to get him to the dinner table. But as time went on, he lost interest in practicing and after eight months, the lessons were dropped. "I guess he just didn't have an aptitude for music," his mother said, "or he would have wanted to practice." She is mistaken. She has confused the rewards to be found in the goal with the rewards (if any) to be found in the efforts to achieve the goal. Jimmy's goal is *playing the guitar*. The fun of making music and entertaining his friends is his goal; practicing is merely the means toward that end; it is not a goal in itself. And practicing is generally not *fun*. It may even, at times, be "punishing."

But hold on a minute! We said the individual tends to repeat those actions which he finds rewarding, and for Jimmy, playing the guitar would have been rewarding. Why did he quit?

The answer to this question is most important to any understanding of child rearing: *The closer in time the reward is to the action, the greater will be the probability of the action being repeated.* The child simply cannot tolerate much delay in rewards. If you offer six-year-old Willie the choice between an ice cream cone this afternoon or a day at the circus next week, his choice won't surprise you. The ice cream cone, *right now*, will win—hands down. (Of course, he may scream his head off next week when he isn't taken to the circus.) We can't expect the child to willingly work for any long-range goals, especially if there are no rewards in the work itself. This is not to say, of course, that he cannot be made to work for those goals which his parents feel are important, but then they are supplying the immediate reinforcement (rewards and/ or punishments) to motivate him.

As the child matures (or better, *if* he matures), he gradually develops the ability to work for delayed rewards. If he doesn't, he faces a bleak future. He may drop out of high school to take a job (usually short-lived) "because I just can't wait to buy a motorcycle." An unfortunately large number of adults have seemingly never developed the self-discipline to tolerate much delay in rewards. Several years ago, a book hit the best-seller lists which presented the author's proven formula for making a fortune in real estate. We doubt, however, that many readers came close to duplicating his bonanza. His method called for years of hard work with no payoff along the way until the ultimate goal was reached. This would be more than most would tolerate.

The rewards in child rearing are also largely long range. Not that there are none to be found along the way—children really can be fun to live with—but when we think of any broad goals in child rearing, we think of the life we are helping the child to attain in his adulthood. If we knew the child would have no life beyond high school, it would be downright cruel to force him to sweat through an arduous class in freshman algebra. The eventual payoff for both parents and child will come years later.

Since the child cannot be expected to be self-motivated to work for these delayed rewards, and may, in fact, not even recognize the eventual goal as rewarding until it is attained, the parents must select the goals as well as provide the motivation. Achieving in junior high school may establish a foundation which will eventually lead to college success, but the seventh grader may not have yet thought of college or see any reason for going. It is all along the way, on a day-by-day basis, that the parents must provide the immediate reinforcement, rewards as well as punishments. Needless to say, this is a task which frequently calls for delay of rewards for the parents: Responsible parenthood is a full-time job.

The *Stimulus* which elicits a response is not the same thing as the motivation for the response, although the two are related. A stimulus (S), as we will be using the term, is some object or energy source in the environment capable of exciting the sense receptors. The sound of the telephone bell excites our hearing receptors; the eardrum, the transmitting bones in the middle ear, and the delicate mechanisms of the inner ear, all react to send a nerve impulse signal to the brain. The bell sound (S) elicits the *Response* (R) of reaching for the telephone receiver. It is that stimulus-response (S-R) association which must be learned. If we had just arrived from a primitive culture and had never before seen or heard a telephone, the ringing bell might elicit *some* response (fear, perhaps), but we would not likely reach for the receiver to answer the call.

There are a number of S-R associations we very deliberately teach our children. We teach him to say "thank you" (R) when Grandmother offers a licorice whip (S). He is taught to withdraw his hand (R) when we point to the kettle and say, "Hot!" (S). Later, he is taught to answer "seven" (R) when asked, "How much is three plus four?" (S). There are many other S-R associations he picks up which we may not intentionally set out to teach him, some desirable and some not so desirable. Mother putting on her coat becomes a stimulus to elicit two-year-old Debbie's tears to go bye-bye. At the sound of running water (S), five-year-old Richard frequently wets his pants (R). The melody of a lullaby Mother sings at bedtime has become the stimulus to elicit the response of sleep for three-year-old Carl. When Marty was eleven, she was injured in a serious automobile accident. At the moment of the crash, a Beatles record was playing on the car radio and they were driving in a dense fog. She is now fifteen. Fear (R) is elicited by automobile riding (S), fog (S), and the music of the Beatles (S).

Children are taught to respond to verbal instructions of parents, teachers, and others in authority. The words of the instructions, however, form only a part of the total stimulus to which the child responds. Only in the simplest S-R associations (such as the reflexive withdrawal of the hand when we accidentally touch a hot stove) is there only a single relevant stimulus present. When we tell the child what to do, the inflection in our voices, the context in which the instructions are given (at the dinner table, out in company, etc.), and perhaps a score of other variables will combine to form a "stimulus complex" acting to elicit the response—whatever the response may be. This fact can help us understand why our instructions may work (i.e., elicit the desired response) one time but not another.

Let's say our intended stimulus is the instruction: "Don't put your elbows on the table." We will call that S_1. We hope the response will be removal of a pair of elbows, and it just may be—maybe. Suppose a situation in which S_2 is a stern voice, S_3 is a table setting in a restaurant, S_4 is the presence of the child's father at the table, and S_5 is the held-out possibility of a fishing trip with Dad tomorrow.

$$S_1$$
$$S_2$$
$$S_3 \longrightarrow R_1$$
$$S_4$$
$$S_5$$

The response, R_1, is a hasty removal from the table of the offending elbows.

But now let's suppose we keep S_1 (the instruction) the same, but change some of the other stimuli.

$$S_1$$
$$S_6$$
$$S_7 \longrightarrow R_2$$
$$S_8$$
$$S_9$$

S_6 is a birthday party setting with five or six friends around the kitchen table. S_7 is Mother's pleasant, almost lighthearted, voice. S_8 is a massive cake with lighted candles waiting to be blown out. And S_9 is the *absence* of Dad from the party. R_2 should surprise no one: *no response* (or at least no removal of elbows).

In the restaurant there was plenty of motivation for R_1. There was the reward of parental approval, but more significant was the fear of punishment: Father's wrath and no fishing trip. At the birthday party, there was less fear of punishment, perhaps none at all, and the *reward* of the fun of breaking rules, doing what the others were doing, etc., sufficient for R_2.

How do we increase the odds in favor of getting that desired response? And achieving it with some consistency?

Here, we need two more concepts of learning: *Drive* (D) and *Habit Strength* (H). Drive is anything which "energizes" us, anything which moves us to action, regardless of what the action may be. Drive gets us moving; where we move depends a lot on learning. If we go all day without a bite to eat, the drive should be high (hunger!). The drive will set off activity of some sort. Just *what* activity will be determined by the relative *habit strengths* (Hs) of a certain number of responses. *Habit strength,* as you have probably guessed, is just what it says. It is a function of *the number of times the particular response has occurred to the particular stimulus in the past.*

The probability of the response occurring is a product of drive (D) and habit strength (H). And we can think of it in numerical terms. Picking arbitrary values, if we give D a potential strength from one to ten and estimate a strength of six to our particular D (the fear of Dad's anger and losing out on the fishing trip) and a strength of 4 in the H of removing the elbows (that is, on four very similar occasions, the elbows came down), we can plug them into the equation $D \times H$ and come up with a probability of the desired response: $6 \times 4 = 24$.

We can easily see what happens as we increase the H. If our young friend had in the past promptly removed his elbows on thirty occasions in a row when asked to do so, the H would be up to thirty. The probability of the desired response has now jumped considerably: $6 \times 30 = 180$, an almost sure bet the elbows will come off at once. The equation makes it obvious that as H increases, D can drop with the probability of response remaining the same. With an H way up at 30, Dad would probably have to do no more than gesture to get the elbows removed. It also follows that if we can increase the D the H can be lower without the result being lowered in probability. (If he were really terrified of the possible penalties for noncompliance, the H for removing elbows might be only 2 or 3 but the odds on obedience would be excellent.)

How do we go about building the H for desirable responses in our children? There are several ways. The child can be "led" through the response (in the manner a golf pro moves the student's arms through the correct swing of the club), he can be encouraged to imitate the response, he can be placed in a structured "learning situation" in which only the desired response is possible (or at least any other is highly improbable), and he can be left to discover the desired response by trial and error with the desired response then being rewarded. The method is not as important as the result. They all will be employed by parents at one time or another, and the rule should be: If it works, use it.

What is most important is that we try to ensure that the child is not building up habit strength for any of a number of *undesirable* responses, since once it is built, it can be awfully hard to tear down. In fact, we never really succeed in reducing a habit strength; the most we can hope to do is build up H for the desired response to a point higher than the H for the undesirable response. When we speak of "unlearning" a response, we really mean learning a competing response. And that is where the work comes in.

For learning to occur, as we have said, the response must be reinforced—rewarded or punished. Most parents have the general idea of reinforcement, a carryover from their childhood, but frequently they find they have "tried everything" and nothing seems to work—not spanking, praise, scolding, ridicule, grounding, bribing, giving privileges, taking them away, reasoning, shouting, or coaxing. Why?

For one thing, the reinforcer may not be effective. If a scolding runs off like water off a duck, the scolding won't be much of a "punishment." If the child has more than an ample allowance and little need for more money, a dollar for each A may not be sufficient "reward."

The reinforcer for the desired response must be greater than the reinforcement he receives for an undesirable response if it is to work. If the rewards found in turning against the parents and following the peer group are stronger in reinforcement value than the punishment meted out by the parents (or the reward of their approval), disobedience can be expected.

We all know children may disobey even when the consequences are drastic. If the reinforcement on the other side is *not* stronger, how do we explain it? Possibly, the delay in reinforcement is too great. *The closer in time the reinforcement is to the response, the stronger will be its effect.* As every parent knows, spanking a child a week or two after an infraction is of little effect. This is true for adults as well as children. The high-living business executive who manages to get roaring drunk at each cocktail party only to moan with a hangover the next morning is a sad example of this law of learning. The rewards of the drunkenness are almost immediate; after only a few drinks, he is feeling "mellow." The "punishment" doesn't hit for several hours. And should he become a full-blown alcoholic, the really severe punishments—loss of job, family, health—will be longer in coming. If he were hit with nausea and a throbbing headache as soon as he took that second drink, he would stop. So-called "aversive therapies" in treatment of alcoholism, antabuse, electric shock, etc. are aimed at bringing the "punishment" closer in time to the drinking, and making the punishment greater than the rewards.

One further phenomenon of learning: *Stimulus and Response Generalization.* Learning a specific response to a specific stimulus wouldn't be of much benefit if stimuli and responses could not generalize. We learn to drive an automobile and the learning generalizes the first time we get behind the wheel of a pickup truck. We may have a bit to learn about truck driving, but we don't have to start from the beginning. Jean, a teen-ager, learns to defy her parents. Her defiance generalizes and she now defies her teachers. Michael, a bright nine-year-old, worked with his father on construction of a ship model. He now tackles an airplane model on his own, and does a better than average job. Bobby, age seven, was bitten by a large German Shepherd. He now fears all dogs. The stimulus has generalized.

Generalization can obviously work to a disadvantage as well as an advantage. As parents, we try to bring about in our children a broad generalization of desirable responses. But we cannot hope to *limit* generalization since generalization is simply a function of the similarity of the generalized stimulus (or response) to the primary S-R. Many years ago, the pioneer American psychologist John B. Watson demonstrated how far a simple conditioned response, fear, can be generalized in a child. He conditioned a little boy, Albert, to fear a rabbit by sounding a loud noise each time the rabbit was brought in. The fear generalized to where Albert showed fear to a woman in a fur coat, a man with a white beard, and several other somewhat similar stimuli. (Watson later, we might add, deconditioned Albert.) If we understand and keep in mind the effect of generalization, it can help us in unraveling some of the "unexplainable" things which happen in child rearing. *Generalization acts like a pebble dropped in a pool. It breaks the water and ripples spread to all shores. Whether the pebble is desirable or undesirable becomes all important.* We can't stop the ripples, but we may be able to influence what pebble is thrown.

The child can be taught to make discriminations as well as generalizations, and he does discriminate. He can learn, for example, that dining in a restaurant calls for behavior quite different from what may be demanded at home, but if the parents permit him to "get away with murder" at the kitchen table, they should expect some generalization when he sits in the restaurant. An undesirable response which has generalized broadly can be very difficult to extinguish, and discriminations are not always easily taught. This is why it is so important to reinforce by reward the desirable primary S-R associations and punish the undesirable S-R associations, and if possible, prevent the latter from being established in the first place. What rewards and what punishments will be effective are the all-important question, and the one which bothers so many parents. In the following chapter, we will discuss what works and what doesn't. First, however, we must decide what we can reasonably expect in the way of behavior and performance from our children. Only if we have established our expectancies and feel sure our expectancies are realistic and justified, can we set about on a program of rewards and punishments, and a program of overall learning, the thing we call child rearing.

So what should be our expectations? Those rather vague abstract goals we mentioned at the beginning of the chapter don't help us a bit in deciding what we want to do with our children. Any goals must be patterned to the individual child and his capabilities, and if the goals are going to provide something to shoot for, they must be broken down into subgoals which are definable and attainable.

"Becoming an educated person" is too broad. Getting an *A* in seventh-grade arithmetic is a goal which can be worked with. We say we want the children to be well behaved when we take them for a drive, but how do we define "well behaved?" If we tell them they are to remain seated and keep their arms inside the car and their voices soft, we have established some criteria of behavior we can deal with. Subgoals which are "operationally definable," that is, have some specific criteria of performance, should be set in every area we decide is important in child rearing. If the child isn't sure what is expected of him, we can't justly punish him for not living up to what we might want.

The goals which can realistically be set are considerably higher than most parents seem to realize. We have heard so many warnings against "pushing" the child, and the supposedly dreadful things which happen to children who "overachieve." With educators and popular child "experts" so strongly dedicated to the comfort of mediocrity, this is to be expected. Parents who demand more of their children and encourage them to achieve are viewed as some sort of monsters bent on turning their children into exhausted, anxiety-ridden neurotics. We do not deny there are parents who make unrealistic demands upon their children and set unrealistic goals for them. But they are in a distinct minority. Most parents and teachers expect too little. And, of course, they get what they expect. The criteria we set for acceptable performance should not be set by the "average" we observe in other children (their parents may expect very little), nor by what the school is willing to accept. It should be established by one thing only: the child's capabilities.

The capabilities can be determined in a number of ways. Let's say we are interested in determining his academic potential. We might look to: 1. Group achievement and "readiness" test given by the schools; 2. Results of individually administered tests of intellectual functioning (IQ); 3. The teacher's evaluation of his potential; 4. The parents' evaluation based upon generalization from other areas; and/or 5. An assessment of his past academic performance.

Number 5, believe it or not, may actually be the best predictor. It may seem fruitless to attempt to judge what he is capable of doing on the basis of what he has done in the past. It may seem we are saying that if Jimmy has been a below-average student in the past, we conclude his capabilities are below average. Not at all. We all know students who have gone along for years, bored and un-motivated, performing below average, who suddenly get turned on to their studies. The marks Jimmy receives are only the tip of the iceberg, and only if we can be sure the tip is representative of the rest of the iceberg can we reasonably say the grades show his potential. Is he working to capacity? Is he free of physical and emotional problems which might hold him back? Has he been given sufficient preparation in previous grades in school?

If we can rule out any and all of these, plus perhaps a few more, perhaps we can say his past school performance is representative of his potential. In most cases, however, this can't easily be done. If there is a question of physical or emotional problems, it calls for professional help which the teachers and school counselors are not equipped to handle. If it is a matter of lack of motivation, then it is probable Jimmy would do much better if fired up. His potential, in other words, is probably higher than his past performance. This determination must be left up to the parents since they probably cannot expect the schools to take much part in it. With all the talk of the supposed dangers of "demanding too much," parents are understandably reluctant to take the necessary steps to motivate their children. To bring the parental foot down and see to it that Jimmy brings home nothing but grades of B or above would be viewed by no small number of teachers as sadistic. But what if Jimmy is capable of achieving A's and B's? Should his parents sit by doing nothing for fear of damaging his tender psyche? If they do, Jimmy may in time begin to see himself as below average—in every way.

There is one way parents can assess capabilities with some degree of accuracy—and probably more than most testing will reveal: They can *accept as present potential, the best performance under optimal conditions.* If a broad jumper averages thirteen feet, seven inches, but on one occasion, a championship track meet in which he was at peak condition and going all out to win, he managed to jump fourteen feet, five inches, we don't speak of him as a 13–7 jumper. Fourteen feet, five inches is his present potential. It may improve in the future, and there may be times he can't reach it, but we do know one thing: He is capable of 14–5.

The evening meal in Jimmy's home is frequently an exercise in frustration. Jimmy picks at his food, complains, refuses to eat a number of foods, spills glasses of milk, and generally manages to turn mealtime into a trial for the entire family. Recently, however, he stayed overnight with a friend. His friend's mother raved over his impeccable manners. "He was a perfect little gentleman the whole time. And his table manners! I just wish we could get our own kids to behave as well and eat as well." Jimmy's parents have a new standard, a new expectancy. They know what he is capable of doing and can demand it.

In school, he has been labeled a "slow reader." His teacher reports he mispronounces easy words, reads with no inflection, and has poor comprehension. One afternoon, however, he went with his mother to the five and ten. He spotted a book on the moon landings and pestered his mother to buy it. She did, even though she felt sure it was beyond his reading level. By the time his father came home from work that evening, the boy had devoured the book and enthusiastically read whole chapters of it aloud to his startled father. Another new picture of his present capabilities, and a new set of expectations.

Are we saying that peak performance, behavior which is optimally motivated and optimally performed, is to be installed as the *expected* behavior? Not exactly. We don't anticipate that it will at once become the present *norm* of behavior. If our broad jumper begins to consistently jump near his own record, we can guess that his potential is now higher. He can now be pushed to go for a new record. Suppose, however, that we praised him each time he jumped within a foot or two of his top mark and awarded him the gold medal for the shorter jumps. What motivation would he have to stretch? *If mediocrity is rewarded, mediocrity will prevail.* It is unrealistic to expect our children (or ourselves) to consistently perform at peak level, but the peak level attained can be employed as the *goal response*, and the goal can be continually evaluated and moved upward as further achievement is observed.

Once we know what the child is capable of doing, why shouldn't we use appropriate means to motivate him toward that goal? Not that we do not accept performance which falls short some of the time. To make the *goal response* the only acceptable response would result in the child seldom "winning" and rather consistently "losing."

But if the *goal response* is kept near the optimal level, the child has the opportunity of finding satisfaction in genuinely *winning*. If the goals are less, he cannot win.

There are several steps in setting goals, determining what you expect from your child:

1. *List the principal goals you have determined for your child's behavior*—at home, in school, chores, toward adults and other children. This is best accomplished by both parents working together, sitting down for some full hours of communication. It should never be done quickly; there are too many areas to cover, and when husband and wife start, they often find they have to re-examine their own values, their areas of agreement and possible disagreement. Since the child is growing and changing, the list must be frequently re-evaluated. Goals are added and dropped, expanded and modified. Then too, the parents' values may change.

2. *Break the goals down into specific subgoals.* This is where it pays to employ "operational definitions" and to be as specific as possible. If the goal is to "take care of his room and his own things," break the goal down into a list of specific goal responses on which he can be judged (e.g., his clothes are to be hung up each night, bed to be made each morning, room to be cleaned Saturday mornings).

3. *List any behavior which you feel needs serious attention.* When facing the challenge of trying to extinguish undesirable S-R associations, we may encounter much difficulty if we have not correctly identified the various learning components. What are the stimuli eliciting the response? Where, when, and under what circumstances is the behavior apt to occur? Is there generalization involved? Have there been past unsuccessful attempts to extinguish it? Why does it seem they have failed? Only when the undesired behavior is pinned down and adequately identified can an effective program of "relearning" be formulated and put into operation.

4. *Establish goal responses for each area of behavior.* No one can tell you what you are to expect from your chil-

dren. Children are individuals. They do not all have the same capabilities or the same prior experiences. Parents are in the best possible position to not only determine what they want for and from their children, but to determine the criteria they wish to set for acceptable performance. Drawing upon what you know of your child, set your goal responses. Then initiate the program toward their attainment.

And now on to the question of just what we, as parents, can do to supply a big part of that essential ingredient: *motivation.*

5

REWARD AND PUNISHMENT
—DOES ANYTHING WORK?

"*Nothing* works! Absolutely nothing! We've tried bribing him. And we've tried beating him. Just nothing reaches that kid."

Are there parents who have not felt this frustration? It is virtually the cry of the species we call parenthood. It is one thing to say what is supposed to get results (and just about everybody seems to have an answer), but what can you do with a child who seems not to have read the book? Is he an exception to all the laws of learning, or is it something else?

Something can be discovered which will motivate a child, that will bring out the behavior and obedience we want. Not just *any* child, and perhaps not *every* child. But then we don't have to worry about every child. It will be enough if we can wisely raise, teach, and control those seated around our own dinner table. Children *are* individuals. This is an obvious observation made much of by the more personalistic child experts. They differ from one another in many ways: age, sex, physical abilities, intellect, interests. They vary both in what they *are* (the genetic endowment they received from their parents) and in what they are becoming. And not one of us with more than one child would think of lumping all children together as if they were so many peas in a pod. With nine very distinct personalities to raise, we can attest to the *uniqueness* of the individual child.

But the idea of uniqueness can be carried just so far. If

every child were wholly unique, child rearing would be impossible. It would come closer to zookeeping. Imagine: If we had a child who responded in almost all ways different from the other children, a child who cried when the others laughed, who turned up his nose at the treats the others clamored for, and in general acted in ways one would never predict, we might, given sufficient time, psych out his strange "uniqueness," but we might go mad in the process, and any activity planned as a family would be a disaster. Human interactions are dependent on our sameness for their success. We rely on the probability that *most* people will respond in similar ways to a given situation, that when we say, "Good morning" to the postman he will not answer, "Drop dead!" that most people will cry when they read or see *Love Story*, laugh at a W. C. Fields movie, and feel elated when they receive a refund from the Internal Revenue.

All children will respond to reward and punishment. The *pleasure/pain* principle applies to all. And, fortunately, the basic half-dozen, more or less, rewards and punishments will almost always include one or more which will motivate any normal child. Some are more effective than others, and some of the popular means employed by parents simply don't work at all.

Rewards. Rewards, as motivators, have a strong appeal. They give good feelings to parents as well as their children. It's fun to make a child feel good, especially when it also results in motivating him to behave as we want him to. It is hardly surprising that rewards, as motivators, have been raised to such a primacy among the members of the pop school of child experts. It all sounds so nice and the parents love it. As we mentioned previously, punishment, any punishment, is viewed as the "rewards only" experts as something dreadful. There is the danger, they claim, of doing irreparable damage to the child's tender psyche if we apply not so tender stimulation to his backside. Punishment will supposedly lower his self-esteem, making him feel both stupid and unloved. It will "block" his ability to learn and grow.

The "rewards only" approach has more appeal than the Super Bowl. And why not? It promises bliss and tranquillity. Child rearing without temper and tears, the answer to every parent's—*and child's*—prayer. Furthermore, it has the ring of psychological sophistication, of humanism and personalism, and of a socially conscious age in which sweetness, kindness, and tender-loving care, we are told, will solve all problems from crime in the streets to gophers in the front lawn.

Rewards can be effective. Many of our actions are motivated by anticipation of some reward, and there are, to be sure, rewards which will motivate a child. Junior may drag his feet dressing for school, but come Saturday morning and a trip to the zoo, and he is apt to set a new speed record. When rewards work as motivators, no parent will choose punishment instead. Rewards are both easier and more pleasant. As a rule, we use rewards when we can, and punishments when we must. If there were no rewards in our day-to-day existence, we might still act responsibly out of fear of punishment, but life would be dismal indeed. Working at a job with no satisfactions other than a paycheck, sticking to it strictly out of fear of starvation, could turn life into a prison sentence. Many of the demands we make on our children both at home and at school are a giant pain in the neck. We admit it isn't all fun, and we are not such fools as to advocate turning the world upside down to make the child's total environment one of fun, since if it were possible, it would be at the price of leaving him unprepared to lead a satisfying adult life. Hopefully, however, his existence will not become wholly unpleasant. We can provide some of his rewards and we can help him find others. For most of us, the average day is filled with countless tasks, both large and small, which give us satisfaction when done well. Some are simply nasty little chores which have to be done. If we don't, we suffer the consequences. Only when we get them out of the way are we free to enjoy the activities we say we work for. We might dream of a never-never land at the end of a Utopian rainbow filled with nothing but rewards, a world in which all jobs are exciting and fulfilling, all activities satisfying, but if we spend time searching for it, we may end up bloodied against a wall of frustration. Ponce de Leon suffered some pretty miserable days in his search for the Fountain of Youth and got only older. Accepting realities, we work for our rewards and we continually seek to increase them. We try to do the same for our children, while at the same time helping them learn that life's satisfactions come with a price tag.

Some of what we speak of as rewards are simply a part of the total environment we want to help create for our children rather than positive reinforcement for specific behavior. These continuing, environmental rewards include the following:

Recognition. The child learns his self-image in large part through praise and recognition (or a lack of it). He looks to his parents in evaluating his own worth, his actions, and his achievements. Praise and recognition become his most significant rewards in early life and remain significant to him throughout his life (sometimes too significant). What husband doesn't enjoy his wife's praise for the shelves he built in the garage? And how often do we hear a wife complain that her husband never pays her any compliments?

Parents seldom need to be told praise is important to their children. They know it from their own needs. Most parents lavish it on their child before the infant is out of diapers. Praise is given when he takes his first step, when he uses the potty properly, when he first says, "Momma" and "Dadda," and when he finally manages to transport the food to his mouth with a spoon. We are all just as well aware of the child's response to praise. The five-year-old presents his mother with a crayon drawing. "Here, Mommie; I made this for you." Of course, his mother oohs and ahs over it. And for the next twenty minutes she is the recipient of a collection of quickly turned out artistic efforts.

To be effective as a motivator, however, praise must be:

1. More rewarding—subjectively, to the child—than the "reward" value of avoiding the task praised.

2. Appropriate. Praise given for subpar performance or for the usually expected everyday acts (e.g., the twelve-year-old brushing his teeth) diminishes the effectiveness of all praise.

3. Compatible with the child's self-image.

Margie's mother tried nagging, scolding, and grounding in an effort to get the teen-ager to keep her room picked up. Nothing had the desired effect. She tried praise. Each time Margie was inspired to make her bed or hang up her clothes, Mother would tell her what a fine job she had done, how nice the room looked, etc. But often as not, the following day the room would be in shambles. Praise didn't seem to work any better than the nagging. Finally, Margie's mother gave up. "I quit. If she wants to live in a pig pen, she can. I'm through keeping after her." A tidy room had apparently little value to Margie. It was easier (i.e., more "rewarding") to let it stay messy. The reinforcement value of the punishments—nagging, scolding, and grounding—was not enough to outweigh the rewards of not doing it. And neither was the anticipated reward of praise.

Margie's younger brother, Kurt, has also been the beneficiary of Mother's program of praise. Eleven-year-old Kurt has been virtually buried in praise. When he has brought home A's and B's on his report card, she has praised him, but she has praised almost as much when he has made C's. He plays with a Little League team, and although he has never made the starting lineup, his mother has repeatedly told him he is the best player on the team. As the praise is given indiscriminately, with no particular relationship to achievement, it has lost its reinforcement value. It is also having a poor effect in terms of how Kurt sees himself. He knows when he has done well in school and that a C is not the equal of an A. He knows there are at least nine other players on the team who can play better baseball than he can. Praise for mediocre performance carries the message: "I think it's the best you can do." Parents frequently tell children, "I don't expect you to get all A's and B's; just do the best you can." But what if the child is capable of earning all A's? Isn't he being told that his parents see him as less capable than he is?

Affection. Being praised for achievement and being loved for achievement are not at all the same, either in what is communicated or in its effect. Yet they are often employed as if they were.

Bestowing affection—loving—as a reward may be effective in the short run, but the long-range effects make it perhaps the least desirable reinforcement. It may motivate the child, but at an awful price.

Affection given as a reward says, "I will love you if you behave as I wish you to behave and achieve what I want you to achieve." Not long ago we overheard a mother gushing over her daughter's piano performance at a sixth-grade graduation tea: "I just love you when you play like that." It may never have occurred to the woman that the remark also says, "If you don't play well, I won't love you."

A child will at times act in "unlovable" ways, just as he will at other times be most "lovable," but to make our love and affection payment for approved behavior is the worst kind of rejection. He isn't loved for himself, only for what he does, and only when he does it.

Affection is important to the child, and we enjoy giving it. Affection, however, should be a sincere expression of our feelings toward the child; it should say: "I love *you.*" Not, "I approve of your behavior." What we intend to communicate in punishment is "I disapprove of what you did." Never, "I dislike *you.*" Obviously, we don't throw our arms around the child who is acting bratty. We punish him. If he has behaved especially well or has achieved at something, we praise him. But affection? We give that "for no special reason" other than to show him how we feel toward him. And because we want to.

Money and Allowances. Adults have learned to work for symbolic rewards (secondary rewards)—money and, ultimately, the things money will buy. As the child matures, he learns to value money. He finds that pieces of paper, currency, can be exchanged for goods and services which have value to him. As a reward to motivate desirable behavior, however, money doesn't work well during most of childhood. There are several reasons why. First of all, most children don't have that much need or desire for money. Occasionally, the child may want some money for something, and he may want whatever it is he hopes to buy so bad he can taste it, but if money is used as a reward for behavior, what will we use during times when he isn't hoping for something? We lose our motivator.

Money rewards are commonly offered for report card grades: A dollar for an A, fifty cents for a B, or whatever the traffic will bear. If we look to what we know of the principles of learning, we can see why it so seldom has the desired effect. Jimmie brings home the report card in June. Whether he has an A or a C in arithmetic will depend on what he did in class on a sunny Wednesday afternoon in April and whether he did his homework on a Monday evening in March when his favorite program was on TV. The reward (or punishment) in June is too far removed in time from the behavior on which the grade is based to have any significant effect.

Money is also somewhat like candy when it comes to reward value. It cannot be used repeatedly. The child will eventually get sick on the candy and lose interest in more nickels and dimes once his immediate desires are set.

Allowances can create other problems. If the parents decide to give an allowance, it should be made clear that it is an allowance and not a payment for sharing in the chores of the household or a reward for good behavior.

We want to teach our children that they owe a responsibility as members of the family, that when they help with the cleaning, yard work, dishes, etc. they are not hired help who should expect a salary. They share in the benefits of the home and are therefore expected to share in the work involved. Paying one of the older children for helping a younger one with his reading or cleaning the garage would communicate something very wrong: That the children are guests or non-paying boarders and we should expect no contribution from them in the way of gratis work. Some parents find the weekly allowance a convenient way to supply the money children need for a variety of things and for "teaching them to save." While we have no strong feelings against the practice so long as it is not tied to payment for chores which should be expected or employed as a reward for good behavior, we have personally never figured out an equitable means of dispensing an allowance and hence have never instigated it. Children have different needs and interests and they vary by age and sex. An amount which would be too little for one child would be too much for another. There are also, we feel, good reasons for not supplying excessive amounts of spending money. We want to know where any money they may have is going and, yes, we reserve the right to some say in how it will be spent, including money they may receive as gifts, etc.

As soon as the allowance is given as a reward for proper behavior, the child is left hanging on a parental hook. If he slips up any time during the week, the funds may be cut off. Again, it is a situation in which the reinforcement is removed in time from the actions. If he doesn't misbehave, is the allowance then a reward for simply *not* acting out of line? If so, it isn't a reward; it's . . .

Bribery. It hardly seems necessary to caution parents against paying bribes to their children, and it wouldn't have been a decade or two ago. But sometimes a bribe can pass as something else, and today there are some of the more fuzzy-thinking child authorities who actually advise it.

Terry is sixteen. He has been in minor scrapes off and on since the fifth grade—cutting school, vandalism, fighting. And a general surliness and rebelliousness. He recently managed to get himself in more serious trouble. It was discovered that he and his friends have been regularly shoplifting from a shopping center. They have also been using drugs. Terry is lucky (?). He hasn't been caught by the law. His parents stumbled across the evidence. They contacted the store owners and made arrangements to make restitution. Then they sought the advice of the school counselor.

Terry has been after his parents for months for a motorcycle. Several of his friends have them, but this has not helped his pleas. His parents, with some sanity, have turned him down. Terry told the counselor of the arguments he has had with his father over the matter. The counselor went to the parents with a suggestion: "Perhaps if you make a deal with him. Tell him if he stays on the right track with no more shoplifting and no more drugs from now until the end of the school year, you will buy him the motorcycle." Fortunately, Terry's parents were smart enough to see where this could lead. They rejected the advice. What would have happened when Terry reached eighteen and decided he wanted a sports car? Would he threaten to hold up gas stations if they didn't buy one for him? Rewarding a child for *not* doing what he has been taught not to do is bribery, and once the child learns he can manipulate for a bribe, his parents may not see an end to it.

Treats and Outings. Most of what has been said of money as a motivator can be said of treats and outings. They don't work very well, at least not consistently.

Psychologists have trained rats with food pellets as rewards, chimpanzees with fruit, and children with candy. But always there is the same problem: When the rat (o.

chimp or child) has had enough, he stops performing. It happens with almost any treat we can think of for a child. At some point, he becomes satiated or loses interest, and the reinforcement value of the reward is lost.

Once in a while treats and outings will work as rewards, but for a limited time only, or only on particular occasions. If the trip to the circus on Saturday is long enough longed for and long enough waited for, young Jimmy may be the model of the perfect little gentleman from Monday on. One problem, however: What do you do for an encore? Slim chance you can offer something to match the circus every week.

If the reward is to be an effective reinforcement and motivator, it must be consistent and almost immediate. This goes for treats, outings, and privileges as well as other reinforcers. You can't offer Jimmy a day at the circus six months away and expect it to keep him on good behavior for half a year. How effective we may expect a promised reward to be will be a function of three variables: 1. Length of delay of the reward (in relation to); 2. Age of the child (in relation to); 3. Desirability of the reward. The more desirable the reward, i.e., the more the child wants it, the longer he may be willing to wait and work for it, but a young child has a short "motivation span." He cannot delay his gratifications for long.

Privileges. These are seldom used as rewards or motivators except as overall rewards for growing maturity and assumption of responsibility. We give Junior the privilege of crossing the street alone when we judge him ready to assume the responsibility. In this sense, we reward him for growing up. These kinds of privileges, however, are probably never given as on-the-spot rewards for acceptable behavior. We don't give Junior the privilege of crossing the street because he brought home a paper from kindergarten with a star on it or because he went all morning without fighting with his sister. *Withdrawal* of privileges, on the other hand, is commonly used as a motivator—"If you're not grown up enough to keep your room clean, you're not old enough to take the car on a date." But this is punishment, not reward.

Punishment. Selecting an appropriate punishment, one which will act to deter the undesirable behavior in the future, calls for imagination and insight. One father of four was perhaps more honest than most of us. He said, "To do a good job as a parent, you have to be a creative sadist." He was not speaking literally, only stating with dramatic candor the problem facing the parent in coming to grips with the question: What punishment will work?

In the perhaps not-so-good old days, the woodshed and the razor strap were the answer to *all* infractions. Simple certainly, but not totally practical in today's complex relationship between parent and child. We're not so sure it always worked in Grandpa's household. Today, an "appropriate" punishment means one which will provide the minimal punishment necessary to alter the behavior, selected with consideration to the overall effect (if any) of the punishment, the age of the child, and the response of the particular child.

Obviously, punishment which cannot be expected to change the child's behavior is not just futile; it *is* sadistic! It smacks of the story of the sheriff of the old West who, putting the noose around the neck of the horse thief, said: "I hope this teaches you a lesson." If punishment is to be used to modify behavior, we must first be relatively certain the behavior *can* be changed.

His mother could not understand five-year-old Arthur's "stubborn bullheadedness." "I just can't figure him out," she told us. "None of my other kids have behaved like him. I tell him to do something, and I never know. One time he may do it, and the next time he may ignore me completely. Just this morning, he was running out to play. I called to him and told him to put on his jacket, but he paid no attention to me at all. I ran after him and, believe me, I handed him a good swat on his little bottom."

Arthur sat in our office, a smiling little guy with a wild shock of red hair. He talked enthusiastically of his brothers and sisters, his friends, and his interests. Then, quite by accident, we stumbled on the key to Arthur's "stubborn bullheadedness." As we were walking behind his chair to the cabinet holding the test materials, we asked him about his favorite TV cartoons. He didn't reply. We stayed behind his chair and asked two or three more questions. He answered once or twice, but apparently did not understand what we were saying. At our suggestion, his mother had his hearing tested. Arthur now wears a hearing aid. He had apparently learned to compensate for a moderate to severe hearing loss with a certain amount of self-taught lip reading. When he wasn't looking at his mother, he often "totally ignored" the voice he could not hear. Unaware of the problem, she had been punishing him for what he could not change.

There are times when any of us may make unrealistic demands on our children. This can easily happen with the first child when the parents have no experience with young children. Parental pride can easily creep in and push parents to push the child beyond his capabilities in toilet training, walking, and the various motor skills. When the child is older, the parents may make academic demands which are unrealistic. Or parents with older children may, unthinkingly, expect all the children in the family, including the youngest, to perform comparably, an expectation which may be unfair to the "baby of the family."

The first rule for punishment should be: *Make certain the behavior demanded is within the child's capabilities.*

The second rule: *Define clearly your criteria for performance.*

We watched a somewhat harassed young mother with her preschooler at a playground. First, she scolded him for throwing sand in the sandbox. Next, she screamed at him for climbing the jungle gym. Then, in series, she scolded and swatted him for going down the slide backward, chasing a little girl, barely missing being struck by an older child on the swing, and squirting water by placing a finger over the spigot of the drinking fountain. We don't know the mother and we do not know how many previous trips to the playground she may have made with her son, but if our guess that this was the first or second trip is correct, then the boy was probably breaking a number of rules he never knew were rules. Who taught him the proper way to go down a slide? Who said sand in a sandbox isn't for throwing? Or that drinking fountains are not for squirting?

We may say, "I'm *sure* he knows better than that, or at least he ought to," but can we be all that sure our children always know what we expect of them? We base the statement on what we think we know of our children, but, as our children are well aware, even parents can be wrong. And we cannot, in fact, always be sure he or she knows the rules of the game—whatever the game may be.

Does this mean we must specify, in exact terms, any and all expected behavior covering any and all situations? Let's hope not. That would be unrealistic, a little like trying to write a law which would be free of loopholes. Fortunately, it is not necessary. What we need is not a voluminous code of laws setting out the exceptions, explanations, and penalties for infractions. What we look for, and demand, is clear and simple: *Obedience*. That's it. Clean, concise, and sane.

Stated so boldly, it sounds harsh, and to say the *only* thing we demand of our children is obedience makes us sound like martinets. It seems so arbitrary, so uncompromising, it is easy to understand why any compassionate parent might look for another answer. But reality cannot be altered without creating serious problems. And the reality is that we *do* demand, then expect, obedience from our children. We cannot, and we feel sure no parents can, hope to specify in advance all rules and expectancies to cover a given situation. But we can specify the behavior we expect *right now*. Our young mother on the playground could probably never in a million years have anticipated all the things her active little boy might get into. It would be impossible for her to give a set of rules before leaving the house. Once at the playground, however, she might have reduced her frustration by giving him the rules as the situations arose. This would have meant close supervision and observation in the beginning (and with a young child, the supervision would probably have to continue during the stay) so that she could catch the undesirable behavior when it started and "nip it in the bud," first by making him aware that it is forbidden, then punishing him if it continued.

State the expected behavior in words the child can understand and with criteria which can be measured. Our courts declare laws void which suffer from vagueness, and there is a maxim in law: "It is better that the law be certain than that it be just." Of course we want to be just in dealing with our children, but justice rests in part on certainty. If we tell Jimmie to be home from his friend's house "early," can we, in justice, punish him for coming home "late?" If we tell him to be home no later than four-thirty, we can justly punish him for coming in at five or even four thirty-five. We might give warning, "If your room isn't cleaned by noon, there'll be no television tonight." Yet if the criteria for a clean room has not been clearly established, we cannot justifiably carry through our punishment. What we consider a clean room and what our teen-agers consider a clean room may be light years apart. If we make clear what we expect, our children will know where they stand, and what they can expect if they fall short of compliance. And it is also clear what it is we are punishing. The punishment is imposed for the *disobedience.* The children may still feel the rule in question is stupid or capricious, but they will at least know where they stand. Once we recognize and they understand it is disobedience we are punishing, we can turn to the very important question of what punishment will be most effective.

Grounding. As a punishment, grounding is of rather recent vintage. Few of us over forty ever heard of grounding when we were young. In those days, most parents took a more direct approach: a slap on the backside, a tongue lashing, or some ingenious physical torture such as standing in a corner for an hour, writing "I will not talk back to my mother" five hundred times, or scrubbing the bathroom tile with a toothbrush. Once in a while we might have been kept inside when we wanted to join our friends at play, but grounding as a selected punishment was rarely employed. Today, grounding may rank first in popularity as a punishment. It has several advantages. First, it's simple. It can be applied in a variety of situations for a variety of infractions and at all ages (except, of course, earliest childhood when then the child is, of necessity, kept pretty well confined). If Willie comes home with a D in history, he is grounded. Mary doesn't clean her room. She finds herself grounded. Jimmie gets the same for breaking a neighbor's window. Grounding can be the punishment to fit all crimes.

Second, grounding permits us to vary the severity of the punishment to better "fit the crime." We can ground the child for an hour, a day, a week, or for several months. If a spanking is going to have the desired effect, it must be given with enough force to really sting. With any less, it may be annoying to the child but not punishing. If it is applied with greater force, it can be brutal or even dangerous. A spanking is also not a punishment which can be extended. Jimmie's parents may be very upset over a broken window, but they are not likely to give him a spanking every day for a week for the broken window.

One further advantage (?) in grounding is the minimum of involvement it demands of the parents. This may account for its popularity. Once the sentence "You're grounded" has been pronounced, the parent doesn't have to do anything other than keep an eye on the door. For parents who can't stand spanking and shy away from verbal whippings, grounding offers a desirable alternative. It can also, at least for a time, ensure against further infractions in situations in which the disobedience occurs when the child goes out. If he misbehaves when outside with his friends, grounding him may not teach him anything, but it does keep him locked in where he will have no opportunity for further trouble.

Many of the advantages in grounding can prove to be disadvantages. Grounding can be handed down in a most capricious manner: "Talk back to me just once more and I'll ground you for the rest of the school year." It is more probable we will apply grounding long after the infraction (thus making the reinforcement ineffectual) and/or after a series of unpunished infractions ("I've told you for the last month to clean your room; it's still a mess, so I'm grounding you for two weeks."), which is a periodic reinforcement and less than effective. There is virtually no criteria for determining severity. If the punishment is to be the minimal amount necessary to deter the behavior in the future, how do we determine how lengthy a grounding will do the job? We usually can't. And this can lead to injustice or ineffectiveness.

Don and Marty are brothers, age thirteen and twelve, and like so many brothers close in age, they have their battles royal. Marty is often the instigator, but the boys' mother takes the stand that "it takes two to make a fight," so when things get out of hand and the boys won't stop when told, she understandably punishes both, usually by grounding them for the day. Still, the fights go on. And the grounding is not strictly equitable. Don is the outdoors type. Whenever he can, he heads out the door to play kick ball with his friends in the street or down to the schoolyard to shoot baskets. Marty, on the other hand, is crazy over model airplanes and is happy spending every free minute with pieces of plastic and a tube of glue. For Don, grounding is the worst of all punishments, but for Marty, it generally means nothing. The equal punishment isn't equal at all. Don is punished, but not Marty, and the grounding is not likely to keep Marty from picking the next fight.

Sending Him to His Room. Everything that can be said of grounding can be said of the "punishment" of banishing the child to his room. It may get him out of your way and out of your hair, but it isn't likely to have much deterrent effect. Generally, it is not punishing. Wouldn't most children rather escape to their room to get away from a bawling out? Besides, while he is confined to his room, he is free of any chores. A friend of ours, mother of two adolescent girls, went through what bordered on an evening ritual. The girls were expected to wash the dishes and tidy up the kitchen. Invariably, it would lead to a screaming argument over who was to do what. After a few minutes of this, their mother would step in and order the girls to their rooms. The girls avoided the work, and their mother avoided a tension headache. But no one could call this a punishment. It was more a manipulation!

The real absurdity of it becomes doubly obvious when we think of the typical child's room. In most homes, he keeps his most cherished possessions in his bedroom, the toys, books, and what have you. Most middle-class youngsters have radios, and a growing number have TV sets in their rooms. With a room which is an entertainment center, what punishment is there in being sent there?

"I Make Him Do It." This is not punishment and should not be included in our discussion of punishments. It is enforcement only. Many parents, however, apparently fail to make the distinction.

Billy's room is beyond belief. Clothes piled on a chair and dropped in the corner. Half-filled cans of pop standing on the dresser top. Paperback books and comics scattered on the bed and under it. There is even a stale, partly eaten bologna sandwich on the night table awaiting an ant invasion. Following a month of demands, pleas, and threats, Billy's mother lowers the boom. She marches the boy to his room. "All right, now I'm going to stand right here while you give this room a thorough cleaning." When she told us of the boy's slovenliness, we asked, "What punishment do you hand out when he doesn't clean it?" "I just make him do it," she replied. "It may get the job done," we told her, "but it isn't punishment." We explained to her that Billy obviously had no interest in a clean room. It was her concern, not his. And she was not providing any motivation. "The next time he turns his room into the city dump, all he has to do is wait out the requests and then, at some point in the future, give in and do what he is made to do and was asked to do in the first place." If his failure to clean the room was punished at once (and the punishment is an effective motivator), things might change; Billy might start keeping it clean.

Taking Away Privileges. Grounding is a deprivation of a privilege, actually a number of privileges—all that the child might want to do outside. *Deprivation* can be applied broadly or narrowly. We can cut off one activity or a whole list. The severity of the punishment can be varied by either the desirability of the activity (the more he enjoys it, the more punishing will be the deprivation) or by the number of privileges taken away.

Deprivation may have motivational value, or it may fail, often for the same reasons. It often taxes our parental ingenuity to come up with a privilege which, if taken away, will be painfully missed. And unless it is, deprivation may not work. Parents used to say, "No dessert," the punishment for unacceptable table manners. But in our house (and we suspect in others as well), dessert isn't always on the menu. Besides, we have some who are not that crazy about desserts. What then?

The big threat today is television. For almost any and all infractions, parents can turn off the tube. Unfortunately, while it is easy enough to flip a switch, it may leave something to be desired as an effective motivation. What if the child isn't a TV addict? Or what if his favorite program doesn't come on until Thursday, and today is only Monday? Taking away the TV privileges can be a workable motivator *if* the loss of TV really *hurts,* and if it can be enforced almost immediately.

This applies to more than just TV. It takes some psyching out to discover what he or she might really *hate* to lose. And it takes some luck in timing to have the infraction occur just when the privilege is coming up. As a whole, the method doesn't work well at all. It can be improved if the parents work at *knowing* what privileges are most desirable to the child. If we are going to use it as a motivator, we have to know them. They are the ones we look to when we think of deprivation.

Verbal Punishment. Scolding is the universal punishment. Even when we impose another punishment— spanking, grounding, or whatever—we usually accompany it with a verbal onslaught. In 99 per cent of homes, each child is scolded at least once, forty-seven out of fifty days. We made up the statistics, but what parent would question them?

Just about all parents scold their children. Some seem to do little else. The scolding takes many forms. At its best, nothing is more powerful as a motivator; at its worst, nothing is less effective.

Frank and Clare are the parents of three boys, ages sixteen, thirteen, and twelve. Richard, their sixteen-year-old, has been a problem since he was in the eighth grade. Nothing serious, but enough trouble in school and at home to add more than a few gray hairs to his parents' heads. The other two boys have been less troublesome, although twelve-year-old Kevin is beginning to show signs of similar acting up.

Clare is strongly opposed to corporal punishment. The boys have never been spanked. Both parents liberally employ scolding—broadly defined. Frank uses a long, drawn-out approach with a 1–2–3–4 logic which backs the child into some sort of "logical" corner and leaves him defenseless. Clare screams at them. And the boys don't pay much attention to either of them. Frank's logic becomes a game of one-upmanship. He seems more set on proving he is smarter than his sons and can "talk them into the ground" (Clare's description) than in simply scolding. Even their youngest sees through it. Clare's screaming is merely a series of short-lived storms the boys weather without noticeable effect.

Paul and Betty have five children, ages eight to fifteen. Betty tries her best to avoid any confrontations with her children. "I can't stand hassles," she says. Her answer to most misbehavior is "Wait until your father comes home."

Bill and Florence have an only son, age fourteen. Florence has a singular method of scolding. She tries to create guilt. No matter what her son, Tony, may have done wrong, she interprets it as an intentional act of hostility directed at her. "How could you have done such a thing to me?" is a question Tony has heard most of his fourteen years. Also, "If you loved me, you'd never do such a thing." If the infraction is somewhat more serious (by her strict standards), she may turn on the tears. Then comes "You are breaking your mother's heart." Bill has tried, without success, to convince his wife that Tony does love her and is not trying, as she claims, to "destroy" her. But her answer is always the same: "My mother always said children will break a mother's heart, and it's true; I'm sure Tony hates me."

For scolding to be an effective motivator and deterrent, the following must be present:

1. *The child must value acceptance by his parents.* He must value being liked, and value their love for him.

2. *He must fear their disapproval.* Most of the fear of scolding stems from the fear of the power of the parent to impose even more feared punishment.

3. *The scolding must have equal force from both parents.* Both parents must be able to administer it, although not necessarily at the same time. What must be avoided is

the strong-parent/weak-parent syndrome in which the child learns to play one off against the other.

4. *The scolding must center on the specific misbehavior.* Shotgunning the scolding to include all the child's past sins is unjust and makes the scolding ineffectual.

5. *The scolding must focus on what the child did, not center on implications of what he is.* It must communicate disapproval of his actions, not disapproval of him as a person.

6. *It must emphasize the desired behavior and clarify the obedience expected in the future.*

7. *The scolding should be administered as soon as the infraction is discovered.*

None of our example parents pass the test. They are not effective scolders. Frank and Clare are planting seeds of rebellion. At some time, the boys will find a way to escape his *I'm-smarter-than-you-are* logic and her screaming. In the meantime, their scoldings breed only resentment without changes in behavior.

Betty has copped out. By passing the buck to her husband, she has cast him in the role of the bad guy, and sadly enough, Paul has accepted it with relish. Despite the enforced "Yes, sirs," however, there is no discipline in the home. The children have more than enough time to do as they please while their father is away. The "unified front" so necessary to parental authority is simply nonexistent.

Florence is a special case of destructive parenthood. Her petty paranoia designed to leave her son stoop-shouldered with guilt is the worst of all scolding. The parent who is obsessed with *receiving* love from her children cannot give love in return. Her method may have the desired effect in terms of obedience for a time, but at a terrible price.

To examine our points of scolding:

If any of us receive a "chewing out" from a policeman, the boss, or our spouse, it is painful because we *fear* criticism and its consequences. It may be fear of loss of status, affection, income, physical pain, or liberty. Whatever, there *is* a fear, and it is fear which makes the scolding an effective motivator and reinforcer. If the child does not fear the scolding, either because of loss of parental approval or a generalized fear response tied to corporal punishment, the scolding will bounce off him with no effect whatsoever.

We said scolding should have equal force from both parents. They don't need to be carbon copies of each other. They shouldn't be. If Father and Mother use exactly the same approach with the children, the children can probably do just as well with only a single parent. Dad may shout when he scolds. Mom may never raise her voice. The force and the effect, however, may be the same. There is more than one way to skin a cat or scold a child. All effectiveness will go out the window, however, if they sit in judgment on one another's method and fail to support one another. This is probably the most common cause of breakdown in discipline. The wife says, "No wonder the children are so upset and rebellious. Their father shouts at them all the time." The husband answers, "How can you expect children to obey when their mother never jumps on them for anything?" In the name of concern for her children, she lets him (*and the children*) know he is doing terrible things to the children with his shouting. He tells her (*and the children*) she is destroying the kids with her permissiveness.

We might be wise to adopt a ground rule in this matter: *Unless there is very clear evidence that what one's spouse is doing to the children is causing them serious physical or moral harm, lay off.* Perhaps the rule will help some of us learn to keep our mouths shut, and learn to back up our co-parent. The last thing in the world any of us want is a spouse who plays head shrinker, judging what we do with our children as to whether it will be psychologically harmful to them. It's bad news in every way. Bad for the marriage, and bad for the children. Usually, our psychological judgments are based on our own experiences in childhood: "I just know it is psychologically destructive to the child's self-image to have a father who shouts at him; my father yelled at me, and I just hated it." We are not our children; they are not us. And we can never be certain their reactions are the same as ours were at that age.

Not that there are no destructive ways to scold. There are. We mentioned scolding directed at the child rather than at his actions. If the child acts in a manner which is stupid and irresponsible, we certainly can point out the stupidity to him. But it is quite another thing, and destructive, to call *him* stupid. Scolding a child for telling a lie is very different in its effect from calling him a liar. A scolding which teaches the child to see himself as bad or inadequate is more than cruel, it is self-defeating. If we teach a child he is no good, we may set up a self-fulfilling prophecy. He may begin to prove to himself we are right about him. ("I'm no good, so how can they expect me to be good?") The scolding is also contradictory: If we really believe he is bad or stupid, why are we scolding him? We can't blame him; it's the way he is, isn't he?

Teaching a child to feel guilt is *always* destructive. We want the child to learn right from wrong and we expect him to feel regret when he doesn't do as he should. But while it is healthy to recognize "I was wrong to do that," it is decidedly unhealthy to feel "I'm a rotten person, and I just proved it again by what I did." Parents have ways of playing on guilt feelings without being aware they are doing so or intending it.

Moralistic scoldings can have this effect. Instead of the parent saying, "If you loved *me* . . ." the admonition is "If you loved God . . ."

Leonard's parents are deeply religious. Both of them were raised in a dogmatic faith which emphasized sin, the pains of hell, and, as a sort of afterthought, redemption. They are raising their son with the same grim prospects. Whenever he steps out of line, the label of "sin" is attached to his behavior. "When you do that, it hurts God." Many times, Leonard has heard his mother say, "That drives the nails deeper into Jesus' hands," and his father say, "When you did that, it made a black stain on your soul." Leonard is now fifteen and is a painfully withdrawn, sad, young man.

When punishment is administered, it should never be tied to a disparagement of the person and his moral worth. The arguments should be rational presentations of why he should or should not have behaved. The scolding should never be tied in with morality in a manner which will brand the child as *bad*. Instead, it should be based on a recognition that the child: 1) was aware of what he should or should not have done, and 2) he made the *choice* of disobeying, but that the scolding extends no further than the action for which he is being scolded. When he slugs his little brother, he is punished because he knew slugging was not permitted and he chose to violate the rule. The punishment goes no further than that. And once it is over, the matter is closed. He should never have to go around feeling unloved.

Spanking. As soon as the child experts decided to wage war on children in the name of a more enlightened psychology, they attacked all corporal punishment as a means of discipline. "It brutalizes the child." "Spanking is sadistic." "You should approach the child with reason, not brute force." Magazines of the thirties were filled with arguments against spanking. Laws were passed outlawing it in the schools. And by the nineteen forties, no "modern" parent would think of spanking a child (or at least admitting to it).

And where were the psychologists while all this was being argued? Some of them abandoned scientific methodology and joined the popular advocates of the no-spanking school. The majority kept their objective heads and studied the behavioral laws of learning. They did not condemn spanking. Most of them didn't even enter the argument. Many parents, however, were left with a different impression. We still encounter parents who are genuinely surprised to find a psychologist who does not condemn spanking.

The facts? There is no evidence a spanking is any more harmful psychologically than physically. A spanking is not child beating. We are all aware that child beating exists and is increasing. But the responsible parent administering a spanking is not going to turn into a child beater, and the child beater is not going to be deterred by those who oppose spanking.

It has been claimed that spanking a child encourages him to act out hostility toward others. There may be some truth in this to the extent that hostility may be displaced. But this is as true of scolding as it is of spanking. We have all seen this in our children. We jump on the child for his misbehavior. He then turns on his younger brother or sister. But there is no evidence this is more likely to occur following a spanking than following any other form of punishment. Hostility is a response to frustration. It is not the only possible response, and it is seldom the best, but it is usually the first response learned by the child (after screaming). As he grows up, we try to teach him other ways of handling his frustrations, and we punish him for his expressions of hostility. Hostility may be encouraged through the example of the parents if Mother and Father have found no other means of handling their own frustrations. But spanking, if the parents are at all mature, is not a reaction to frustration (although we may be very frustrated and angry when we spank); it is a means of discipline. Which brings up another point:

We have all heard "You should never spank the child when you are angry." Think of it for a minute. If our children disobey, won't they expect it will anger their parents? If we spank right then, we will be spanking in anger. We are not, we might add, masochists; who would want to have to spank without anger? The whole purpose of giving reward and/or punishment is *learning*. Shouldn't the child learn that if one acts in undesirable ways, people— parents, teachers, bosses, neighbors—may become angry?

We are also told, "Since the child can't hit back, spanking exploits him." This is a relatively new argument. We hear a lot of talk of "exploitation" in a wide variety of human interactions. It is quickly becoming a banner cliché. Certainly spanking is *imposed* on the child and the child can't fight back. If he is big enough to turn it into a slug fest, we should find some other means of punishing. We make him do his homework, and he can't fight back. We send him to bed at a reasonable hour and he cannot retaliate. And so on, and so on. If spanking is exploitation, then child rearing in which the parent plays a responsible role is exploitation.

Spanking should have limits, however. It should probably never be carried on beyond early childhood. When the child reaches adolescence, spanking is a painful humiliation, and the idea in any punishment is to deter certain behavior and to teach different actions. It should never be done to humiliate.

Basic Hints for Reward-Punishment. 1. *Make sure it works.* Test out the reward or punishment. If it doesn't work, discard it, but make sure you give it a proper test.

2. *Use only the mimimum amount necessary to bring about change.* Heaping on either reward or punishment is a psychological overkill. In time, it either loses its effect or becomes cruel.

3. *Don't use unenforceable threats or bluffs.* Those fly-off-the-handle threats ("If I have to tell you to pick up your socks one more time, I'll take away all television for a year!") set up a game in which the parent loses. The child knows the threat is a hollow one, and he may conclude parents are all talk, nothing more. If you use a threat, make sure it is a promise: Be prepared to carry it out.

4. *Reinforcement must be consistent or it may have a reverse effect.* Most of us have to be burned more than once to learn hot objects are to be avoided. It would take many more times if the hot object burned us one time

but not the next. Any reinforcement—reward or punishment—which is administered in a periodic fashion not only will fail as a motivator and reinforcer, it may just backfire. The child may learn just the opposite of what we desire. The key to all reward and punishment in child rearing is consistency. It must be given each and every time.

5. *The closer in time the reinforcement is to the action reinforced, the better the result.* Reinforcement given an hour after the action is less effective than if given immediately. A day later, and it is much less effective. It may not be convenient to give the reward or punishment at once; it may even, in the case of punishment, be very embarrassing, but if we want it to be effective, that's what is demanded.

6. *No one reward or punishment will work with all children or with one child at all times, for all actions, or at all ages.* What will work best comes down to trial and error, parental good sense, and the willingness to stay flexible. Communication between the parents in which they share their observations helps. Communication with the child is essential to success. Then, we use whatever works best.

6

CONVERSATION AND COMMUNICATION

Tom Lehrer, the comic, does a routine in which he talks about the current obsession with "breakdowns in communication." "If they can't communicate," he says, "the least they can do is *shut up!*"

He may have a point. At times it seems we are in danger of burying ourselves in meaningless rhetoric about "meaningful communication"—or the lack of it. It has become one of the sacred cows of the child-rearing mystique. Mothers who haven't discussed anything more profound than rising food prices with their husbands for years wring their hands in anguish over a failure to communicate deeply with their children. School administrators, in a high priority effort to "relate" and establish "lines of communication" with the students, are setting up all-day "rap sessions." We need their help and suggestions. It is, after all, their education, and they should have a say in it. By all means! The suggestions which came from one such junior high group (duly and seriously noted by the teachers) included the firing of all teachers over thirty, a vote in the hiring of faculty, and the elimination of all math and history. A teacher who participated told us she felt the session was "very fruitful." A student described it as "crap."

If they didn't have enough reason for developing tension headaches, parents were given one more with the publication of a best-selling book on parent-child relations which told the parent readers they must learn to converse with their children in a psychological language expressive of empathy and acceptance, something called "childrenese." It really isn't hard to learn if you are used to talking to your children like a non-directive psychotherapist. But whatever you do, don't expect your children to speak *your* language; it's your obligation to learn childrenese. Of course, someday we expect that child to live in the adult world, but perhaps by then he will be fortunate enough to have a boss or an army sergeant who has been trained in childrenese.

Why now do we hear so much talk of a "communication gap" between parents and their children? Is it really a new problem? We didn't hear any similar expressions of concern when we were young. Could this have been because we communicated better with our parents, or because no one, least of all our parents, seemed to care much whether we communicated or not? Or is it possible we have so recently become aware of a serious problem which has been undetected in previous generations? And is the communication gap a part of that much talked about greater problem: *The Generation Gap?*

Perhaps it would be an important first step if we admitted what we are talking about. When most adolescents complain, "I can't communicate with my parents," they mean, "I can't get them to accept my views and go along with what I want." When parents say, "We can't communicate with our children," they mean, "They ignore our opinions and they won't tell us what they are thinking and doing." If these loggerhead positions represent a communication gap, then we can certainly agree there is a sizable communications gap in many homes. Furthermore, the gap isn't just between parents and teen-agers. It shows up between the parents, and between parents and young children.

If we remember our childhood, we know communication is not a new problem. But as with so much else, there is a difference. For one thing, parent-child dialogue has been given a new status. Adults have repeatedly told one another our generation must listen to "the voices of the young." The over-thirty generation, so the line goes, has made an incredible mess of virtually everything. We have been the creators of war, pollution, poverty, and pesticides. We are obsessed with materialism, devoid of morals, and ignorant of the great universal truths so evident to our children. We have handed a dreadful legacy to our sons and daughters, they say. And lacking the clear vision, expanded knowledge, and shining idealism of the "Now" generation, we must look to them to save the world—and grant us redemption. One community sponsored a series of panel discussions for adults. The panel tackled changes in the schools, drug laws, child-rearing practices, ecology, and the new morality. The panel members were drawn from among the students at the local high school! In introducing the panel, the school board superintendent told the assembled parents: "We must begin to listen to our youth, to draw upon their insights." A middle-aged father who attended the discussions told us: "It makes sense to have the kids put on something like this; I don't think we have anything to offer them." Maybe *he* doesn't. But he doesn't speak for us, and we do not believe all parents are willing to terminate their roles in a whimper of inadequacy. Perhaps, just perhaps, one reason so many children complain that their parents don't listen to them is that so many of their parents' generation have told them they are deserving of rapt attention each and every time they tell their parents what to do and each time they offer a solution to any of the score of problems they are convinced we, their elders, have created, and they don't always get the attention to which they are entitled.

We may not be able to do anything about the popular adult sport of self-flagellation. Some adults seemingly get their kicks out of a collective guilt. They accept the blame for everything from the assassination of John Kennedy to the exploitation of the American Indian. We have no intention of joining their masochistic cult, thank you. We did not create all the problems of the past four hundred years, nor all the problems˙ of the past decade. And we have seen little evidence which would convince us that the younger generation has uncovered cures for all the world's ills. Yes, we want to hear their opinions. We will listen to what they have to say, and expect the same courtesy from them, but we are not yet ready to place a halo on the brow of youth or install teen-agers as our oracles.

Another thing accounting for the emphasis on a communication gap is the realistic fear parents experience as they become aware of the growing problems of drugs, rebellion, sex, etc. among children at even a grade school level. Our parents might have been able to relax, secure in the knowledge we were "running around with a pretty good gang." That isn't enough today. Parents very much want to know what their children are doing—and thinking. If we could all be sure what is going on inside our children's heads, we could either rest easy or take action. As it is, if we can't communicate well with them, we are left to wonder and worry. Even if our children do open up, we may not learn much. Certainly, we are not going to find out everything. Children tell their parents just so much and no more. That's one thing which hasn't changed.

With the popular child experts, the emphasis is on parents understanding their children. Little is ever said about children learning to listen to and understand their parents. One more reversal of rational order! We enjoy our children. Since we enjoy them, we enjoy hearing their views. They are truly very interesting, exciting persons, and it is fun sharing ideas with them. We want to understand them and the world in which they live, and it is important that we attempt at all times to do so if we are to do our job as parents. But let's talk sense: It is even more important that our children understand what their parents are thinking and saying. We have the responsibility of providing them with answers, giving guidance, and setting an example of rational living. They look to us for this, and it is important they understand what we are saying and doing. They have to know what is expected of them and what the limits are. When we read what these experts are saying, we might ask, "Just who is running the show?"

Communication is a learned skill. It can be developed only through practice, and good communication will never be established overnight. Ideally, it should begin to develop as soon as the child starts to talk, but speaking realistically, we all know things have a way of slipping by and parents frequently find they are living with a child they don't know as well as they might like—or as well as they should. When this has occurred, it is not always easy to re-establish those "lines of communication." Remember, communication may be far more important to you than to your child. He has his friends to talk with, and they share common interests, so conversing with his parents may not be one of his "needs." He can tell you what he wants without having to reveal much of himself at all, and if he doesn't look on his parents as friends, he will probably keep things pretty much to himself—much to the frustration of his parents.

The following are basic guidelines which have been found to be effective. They might be called "practice rules."

1. *Establish family conversation times.* If we want our children to develop an interest in reading, we should be reading ourselves. If we want to build communication with them, their parents should be talking to one another as well as to them. The all-too-familiar family in which the husband spends his evenings in front of the television and the wife does her own thing in some other part of the house with little ever exchanged between them, is not likely to be a family in which parent-child communication is developed. We may attempt to explain it by saying, "I'm just not much of a talker," an excuse used by more men than women, but if the need for family communication is recognized, the copout will be discarded and some

concentrated work put into developing conversational skills. It is simply too important to ignore.

In counseling married couples, we generally advise them to set aside a period of time, two or three hours each day, for husband-wife talking. At first, many couples claim it is impossible. They either do not have that much free time or they can't come up with enough to talk about for that length of time. And, of course, many parents find difficulty sitting down to talk without repeated interruptions. Granted, it takes planning and practice before the stumbling blocks are eliminated, but with enough motivation, it can usually be done. And in order to develop the sort of marriages and families most of us want, it is absolutely essential. Virtually everything of value between husband and wife rests on good communication, and the same can be said of parent-child relations. To attempt to communicate in a crisis situation, when communication skills have not been developed through daily practice, can often make matters worse.

It is every bit as important to establish times for family communication in which all members of the family can share experiences and views. In most families, the evening meal was more or less the traditional time, but this has been lessened in many homes in recent years. Fathers work late, parents are in a hurry to be off to evening activities, and an increasing number of parents find it easier on their nervous and digestive systems to feed the children early and have a leisurely meal together in peace. Sanity and sound behavior can be established, however, which will make the family meal enjoyable for all.

The most common pitfall: You can have family dinner conversation or you can demand the children eat in silence while the parents talk to one another. But you cannot have both. During the family meal is a poor time for Mother to discuss the malfunctioning washer or for Father to relate the latest complexity of office politics. If they try, they find the children going off on their own conversational tangents, often ending up in squabbles. For the sake of everyone, especially parents, husband-wife conversations are best left to later.

It is also wise if you have more than one child to supervise the order of talking. When children have something to share, they usually can hardly wait to get it out. With three or four children (or more!) this can lead to everyone stepping on everyone else's toes with constant interruptions. This can be eliminated if one of the parents acts as moderator, calling on each child in turn to share experiences or views (and calling "time" if he or she goes on too long).

If you live close enough to the school, or if Mother can pick them up and take them back, coming home for lunch can also provide an excellent time for family conversation. If they regularly eat at school, you may still plan a lunch at home once or twice a week, one that can be turned into a mini-party with special treats.

The important point is that regular times be established for family conversation. Without planning, it generally doesn't happen. Everyone gets busy with individual activities and family gathering for conversation becomes very much a chance occurrence.

2. *Let them know you want to hear what they have to say.* Many children are sure their parents have no interest whatsoever in them or their opinions. And they just may be right. Children can be boring as well as interesting, and when they are boring, it is hard not to shut them off, something we cannot always do with a gabby neighbor. Children may want to share their experiences and insights. And when they want to, they *really* want to. And we want to know what they are thinking and doing. But it may call upon all our parental patience to sit through a detailed description of the fourth-grade play rehearsal or the latest rock album. (Dad's problems at the office or Mother's frustrations at the supermarket are no doubt equally boring to the children.)

To communicate a genuine interest in the world of our children, we have to fight back the urge to "take over." It is an all-too-common parental sin. Being "older and wiser," we jump into whatever they are bringing to share with us and at once beat them over the head with our opinions and expertise, often before they have had the chance to fully express their views. They may have information and opinions which are far off base. (Our own views, for that matter, may not always be the soundest.) But unless they are encouraged to express them without fear of being jumped on, they will soon learn to keep them to themselves. The parental "put-down" is as much as anything else what our children complain of when they speak of a generation gap. There is a gap between the generations. Our children are not living in our world, and they are being raised in a world quite different from the world of our childhood. Their tastes in music, dress, and art, their fads, heroes, and favorite TV programs may not be ours. But we should not forget how important they are to *them.* They are a part of their total personality and identity. Putting down their music as "just a lot of noise" is a put-down of *them.* It says, in effect, "You must be stupid if you enjoy that sort of noise!"

If the parent holds strong opinions, regardless of the area, it can be difficult to remain silent when the child holds contrary views. To be honest about it, we all want our children to accept our tastes and opinions even if we say we don't and claim we want them to think for themselves. None of us, however, want our children to become mere extensions of ourselves. To develop in their own right, they must learn to explore ideas and preferences, and if we hope to communicate with them, we must exercise the self-discipline of keeping our mouth shut when they express them. We don't have to agree with what they say; we can express our own, sometimes opposing views. The rule, however, should be the same that we would, in courtesy, apply in conversation with an adult neighbor: We give him the right to his opinion and the privilege of expressing it. We don't interrupt him before he has ten words out of his mouth; and we don't tell him he is stupid or bad for holding such views. Parental guidance doesn't necessitate the use of a verbal club.

3. *Answer their questions. Fully.* We are repeating ourselves, but this is important enough to bear repetition. Children, understandably, want adults to level with them, and the adults often do not do so. By the time many children reach adolescence, they have developed a suspicion and cynicism reflective of just how much the adults in their lives have evaded their questions or have answered them in half-truths. There is a credibility gap between children and adults a mile wide. And why not? They have listened to lies in their schools and too often in their homes for as many years as they can remember. In talking to school age groups, we have found it necessary to exclude all other adults, teachers, youth group leaders, and even other parents, and to attempt to carefully (and sometimes slowly) structure ground rules of honesty and confidence before the group members will open up at all. This is particularly so when we are to discuss the more loaded areas of sex and drugs, but it applies in part to any discussion. First, we have to convince them we are willing to answer any and all questions within our knowledge, no limits, no holds barred. What they say will not be taken back to the adults to be used against them. We respect their confidence. We also have to try to communicate to them that we are not going to react with moral judgment or shock to whatever they bring up. They want answers; we try to give them. We then count on a period of "testing." They ask some initial questions which seem to say, "All right, you said there would be no restrictions or limitations; now let's see if you meant it—or if you are like the rest of the older generation." The questions are never subtle or guarded. They are designed to test the limits, to put the adult on the spot, to see if that wall adults raise to keep out the young and prevent them from discovering the clay feet of their elders will indeed come down and stay down. "Did you and your wife have sex before you married?" "Have you ever smoked pot?" "Have any of your kids

ever been in any trouble?" If they pick up any indications of evasion, anything which says, "That question is
out of line; we won't answer it," they will retreat behind a
screen, and communication will disintegrate into a verbal
game of hide-and-go-seek.

It is hard for us to come up with a question a child might
ask which is not deserving of an honest and complete
answer. There may be such questions, but they escape us.
Nor can we subscribe to that timeworn view that the
answers we give a child must be carefully censured and
strictly limited in information by the child's age: "Tell him
just so much as is necessary at that age; no more." Why?
It may be significant as well as interesting that this oft-
quoted injunction only applies to sex. The six-year-old
may have difficulty understanding a complete, detailed
answer (although this may be more owing to deficiency in
communication skills and embarrassment on the part of
parents than immaturity on the part of the child), but this
warrants evasiveness. If he doesn't quite get all of it, he
will ask further questions. And you can at least feel satisfied
you have maintained the honesty and candor so necessary
to parent-child communication.

4. *Allow for private conversation times.* As important
as family conversations are, there is still need for one-to-one
conversation between parent and child. It becomes increasingly important as the child reaches adolescence.
There are bound to be opinions, feelings, and experiences
which he or she won't want spread before all other family
members.

With more than one child in the home, these private
conversations call for planning. With several children,
strategic planning. Parent-child conversations, as well as
husband-wife conversations, frequently take place in a
setting of repeated interruptions—other children, spouse,
telephone, and assorted chores and activities. Too often,
we converse with children on the run while going about
meal preparation, bedmaking and TV viewing. And we
too frequently sprinkle the conversation with "I'm busy

right now; catch me later." About the only times many parent-child conversations are planned and structured as one-to-one without interference is when the parent is going to lower the boom—"Come in here and sit down; I want to talk to you." What follows isn't a conversation; it's a monologue.

We find shopping trips provide a good opportunity for one-to-one conversations. Not necessarily major shopping expeditions. Those thirty-minute trips to the market can allow valuable time in which to open up to each other. And a shopping trip for new clothes with time out for a soft drink or a snack gives parent and child a chance to really re-establish where you are toward one another and the world of each of you. Time, as we all know well, has a way of escaping us, and a child may undergo many transitions in thought and feeling in a month or two. Unless there are frequent sessions which provide the opportunity to catch up with one another, you can quickly find yourself out of touch with the world of your child.

If you have only younger ones and only one parent home at the time, you probably cannot get away without taking all of them along, but those times when one of you can baby-sit the others, you can make it a parent-and-one-child trip. This can, of course, raise the question of competition to see who gets to go along. We have found it does not need to be a problem if we don't establish a practice of all the children going along each time. Simply let them take turns, with their parent deciding whose turn it is each time.

Fathers, every bit as much as mothers, should take advantage of these times. And the talks should be father-daughter as well as father-son. No one needs to be told what has happened to fathers in this society of ours. They have all but vanished. Overwhelmingly, dads have become males who leave for work in the morning, come home in the evening, stay busy on weekends, occasionally holler at their kids, and pay the bills. Psychologists pin the blame on mothers; sociologists point the finger at the demands of corporate employers. The fact remains: Fathers have a responsibility to be fathers, not in absentia, not through their wives, and not from the role of star boarder or "final authority." The young speak of the "need for involvement," and nowhere can we find a greater need for involvement than that fathers become involved *as fathers* to their children. A child, boy or girl, should feel as free to go to one parent as to the other, to talk openly with Dad as well as with Mother.

5. *Don't shotgun the conversation.* Most of us have the habit of digressing all over the place when we converse. We start with one topic, and within fifteen minutes we have touched on a dozen others. If communication is to result from our conversation, it should be approached somewhat like the warm-up volleys for a tennis match. You can't serve or return more than one ball at a time. And throwing a dozen topics into the conversational hopper never leads to the resolution of even a single one.

The rule is especially important if the topic is an important one and some decision is called for. Many of us are guilty of using an unfair tactic when we come to discuss a "loaded" point with our children (we may do the same thing in talking to our spouse): We throw in everything but the proverbial kitchen sink. We bring up offenses spanning the lifetime of the child in order to prove our point of criticism or justify why we are turning down whatever he is requesting. If there are several points to be brought up and it cannot be shown that they are necessarily associated, take them up one at a time; settle one before going on to another. Otherwise, it muddies up the conversational waters and makes communications impossible.

6. *Keep your parental cool.* The expert who first told parents to never discipline their children when angry obviously never raised children. Of course we become angry, and when we do we may lash out. But our sense of justice may go out the window if we attempt a discussion at such times. If we are to act as responsible parents, we have to learn to let reason prevail over passions. Trying to com-

municate in an atmosphere of anger is more than possibly unjust; it is futile. As the anger increases, a deafness to what the other person is saying also increases. If the emotion is high, for either parent or child, it may be best to postpone the discussion. If it simply can't be put off, the parent can at least bring the emotions under control enough to keep the conversation rational. We may not always succeed in cooling down a child, but parents are assumed to be more mature than their children, and self-control goes hand in hand with maturity.

7. *Keep your parental distance.* Children do not need —or want—parents who intrude too far into their private world. They have a world of their own which should be respected. There are some fine lines, however, which have to be drawn in this matter. Later, in discussing some of the problems in the current youth scene, we will consider the matter of privacy—how much, and in what matters —and how it may and may not conflict with the parental responsibility to observe what is going on in the daily life of the child.

The child's private world may be a source of anxiety for parents. Perhaps we should say it *will* be. We want to know what they are thinking, and especially what they are doing. We can seldom find out, however, by *demanding* they reveal all. Nor can we find out by attempts to worm our way into their world, by trying to become a member of their "club." Prying parents are the arch pain in the neck to children, and the older the child, the more they are resented. Children understandably want to be able to talk together and share interests without the presence of a hovering adult, and most certainly without an adult who repeatedly attempts to join in. Supervise? Yes. Observe what they are doing, who their friends are, and the attitudes they express. But steer clear of invading.

To further clarify the point: We are not siding with those who overemphasize the child's need for privacy to the exclusion of parents, who tell parents they have no business entering into what their children may be doing—

at all. The child may want to be left alone to "do his own thing" and mark every area of his existence "off limits" to adults. Some current experts are willing to go all the way with this: "The child has a right to privacy; his room should never be entered without permission. Parents should never eavesdrop on their children's conversations, etc." Well and good, but what if he and his friends are smoking pot in his room, or his sister is entertaining her boy friend behind her locked bedroom door? How far are parents to carry the business of privacy? We most certainly suggest parents not listen in on the extension to the child's phone conversations nor burst in when the child is dressing, reading or whatever, but it would be plain stupid to shut our eyes and ears to everything and anything which might or might not be going on. Parents can keep aware without prying and demanding the child open all doors, emotionally as well as physically.

8. *Set limits on behavior, not opinions.* This, we feel sure, is the most important point of all. When we have analyzed what goes on in our own family, we have concluded: 1. Ours is a very permissive home, and 2. Ours is a non-permissive, authoritative home. We are permissive in that we permit a very free expression of opinion (limited only by the rules of courtesy—which apply to parents as well as children). They know they can express views on any subject, regardless of whether those views agree with those of their parents. We may, and we do, debate points of view, but the debate is on the level of "equals": They can express their opinions without fear of being beaten over the head with a "shut up and listen to your parents." We may, during the course of the discussion, succeed in bringing them around to our side; we may not. They may convince us of their position.

Our home is decidedly *non*-permissive, however, when it comes to actions. The rule is: You can state your opinions, your convictions, your likes and dislikes; we are willing to listen, consider the matter and discuss it. We will not, however, enter into a prolonged debate leading nowhere. Once a decision is made—after consideration of what they have to present—that's *it*. If our nine-year-old doesn't care for cooked cabbage, we want him to feel free to express it, but once he has it off his chest, we see no reason to permit him to go on endlessly telling the other family members how much he hates it. We are not hung up on the notion that a child should clean his plate each and every time, but if, after stating his likes and/or dislikes he is told to eat it, we expect *compliance*.

As the child gets older, he or she becomes more assertive with each passing year. He wants to try out his ideas, to test his muscles. This is his way of progressing toward an adult autonomy. If he can't express them at home without fear of being stepped on, he will build and maintain a wall which will very effectively shut out his parent. By "asserting himself" we do not mean an unbridled right to tell off his parents. We are still the parents, and rudeness is not permitted. Furthermore, there is a clear distinction drawn between *verbal* assertion and behavior. Some parents seem to draw a distinction, but it comes out in reverse: They don't allow their children to open their mouths, yet they permit them to do just about as they please.

9. *Share your thoughts, opinions, experiences, and dreams with them.* Communication is always a two-way street or it isn't communication. Parents can become fixated on "drawing the child out" and overlook the importance of sharing. He wants to know about your world. You both want and *need* to know about his. Parents don't need to fear exposure and if they are secure, they won't. Let him know that you have felt the feelings he is having, that you have had experiences similar to his, that you make mistakes, suffer disappointments, achieve successes large and small, and still dream idle dreams.

There is a big plus bonus which comes from developing good communication with your children: Children have not yet learned to play the subtle defensive verbal games so popular with adults. When you communicate closely with a child, you won't hear the mindless inanities of the cocktail party. You won't be forced to fight boredom while listening to an endless string of clichés and banalities. We have discovered, in fact, that our children, and other children as well, are, as a group and individually, truly refreshing conversationalists. And in the adult world, such people are indeed rare.

7

THE SCHOOLS:
THEIR GOALS OR OURS?

Once upon a time we sent children off to school when they reached about six years of age. They started in first grade. Then along came some educators who decided they weren't ready for first grade, that they needed kindergarten to prepare them through "reading readiness," "numbers readiness," and "social readiness" programs. But that wasn't enough. Soon the educators decided children were in need of educational and social grooming for kindergarten. So now we have prekindergartens, nursery schools, Montesorri preschools and a whole spate of cradle-to-first-grade, baby-sitting-cum-education institutes. Having started them as soon as we could get them out of diapers, we then set about to extend their school years far into adulthood. College became the continuation of high school and a preliminary to graduate school. We can now find twenty-six-year-olds who have accumulated twenty-three years of something called *education*.

And what we call education today is boring students, frustrating their parents, and confusing just about everyone. What goes on inside the chrome-plated, high tax-supported, modern plastic version of the little red schoolhouse is a mind-boggling misapplication of non-scientific methodology presented in a rhetoric of obfuscation.

Confusion begins when we try to discover some purpose to what children are subjected to in the name of education. Everybody involved in the business seems to have answers.

But *what* answers! Some see education as a group psycho-therapy course aimed at "adjustment." Others want it aimed at solving all social problems from unwed pregnancies to pollution. And still others hold up the lofty goal of "education for the sake of education."

For parents trying to raise their children to some sort of satisfying adulthood, however, the answers the educators present don't even touch on what the parents expect for their children. The answers may satisfy the social needs of the teachers, but they don't help clear up the confusion of either the parents or the students, nor do they have a great deal to do with the all-important goals of the individual child's education. We don't send our children to school simply to have a "learning experience" and we don't think other parents do. We send them to learn those things which will prepare them to live in an adult world and to achieve the goals they will eventually decide upon in that adult world. We don't expect them to set their adult goals when they are eleven years old, nor are we setting their adult goals for them. We don't expect them to figure out what information and what skills they will need in order to live and function happily and productively in that future world. We do expect, however, they will have the opportunity to gain the knowledge and skills which will make it possible for them to make a vocational choice when they are older and to feel confident they have acquired the fundamental education necessary to pursue their choice of vocation.

When some of us were children, our parents and teachers believed we should be taught the "basics"—reading and writing skills, mathematics, science, history, geography, etc. Today, educators tell us these basics are still stressed in the schools. Furthermore, they claim that, thanks to "advanced" methodology, our children are even better grounded in the basic subjects. One wonders. There are, even the teachers will admit, only a certain number of hours in a school day, and the hours have not been extended from the time of our youth. Yet today, the curriculum has been gloriously broadened to include everything from scuba diving to yoga. Required subjects have been added at the drop of a legislative motion, most have been based on:

Educational Myth No. 1: Education is the answer to all social ills. Someone—a legislator, school board member, or concerned parent—becomes alarmed at the increasing drug use among children. A program of drug education is proposed: *If children are made aware of the evils of drugs, they won't try them.* True? Probably not. It has long been recognized that there is a drug problem in the medical and nursing professions. Not that a sizable number of doctors and nurses are misusing drugs, but the fact that some of them are and that these are members of professions who are the most knowledgeable of the danger would raise the obvious question: How much does education deter drug abuse? Or what about alcohol education? Who knows more of the sad results of overdrinking than an alcoholic, but does it stop him from drinking? A front-page story tells of the rise in unwed pregnancies among high school girls and the spreading epidemic of venereal disease. We add a course in sex education. Alas, the rates continue to rise. Kids who know more of contraceptives at thirteen than their parents did at twenty-five are checking into maternity wards. Or take driver training. Teen-agers are killing themselves and others on the highways at an appalling rate. Does driver training significantly reduce the carnage? No one seems able to show that it does. But then, we don't run any empirical studies, examine the data, and either keep the program or throw it out on the basis of results. What if it were discovered that the programs don't do what the educators hope they will do? All those driver-training cars donated by the automobile agencies might have to be placed on a used car lot or turned into taxis. And what would become of those miles and miles of sex education films showing little ping-pong balls scurrying through the plumbing network? We might even find school nurses going back to nursing, physical education instructors back on the basketball courts, and industrial arts teachers deprived of their afternoon drive in the countryside. The notion that education ensures against foolish, irresponsible, and even dangerous choices is wishful thinking. The suggestion that we set about to cure our social ills through classroom instruction borders on idiocy.

Are we opposed to our children learning of sex, drugs, the proper driving of an automobile, or any of the number of other such required subjects? Certainly not. We also have no objection to their learning to ride a horse, dive for abalone, or play chess. We only question whether the classroom is where they should learn it. And this isn't to say that we are clinging to the old argument that sex being such a "delicate" area should be handled by a one-to-one parent interaction only any more than the subject of drugs or automobile driving must be placed only within a very "special" context. We do question whether school-time allocated to this purpose is a proper use of the class-room hours. And we reject Educational Myth No. 1.

Educational Myth No. 2: Happiness and success are directly related to the number of years spent in classrooms. Are children who go through nursery school better adjusted adults or happier teen-agers than those who didn't have this "advantage?" Does two years spent in a junior college better prepare one to cope with the pressures and challenges of suburbia? Do all of those endless hours spent in classrooms and labs add up to the production of a saner human being? Even a self-satisfied one? For quite a few years now, the schools have been selling and the public has been buying the myth that schooling leads to better adjustment in one's personal life, that the more notches one can carve in an academic belt, the higher one is apt to score on an examination of mental health. So we encourage youngsters who might become good hod carriers but who could never learn an algebraic equation to sit through filling-time courses, watered down to the youngsters' level with a heavy emphasis on "adjustment" until they have served a four-year sentence and are handed high school diplomas signifying *what?* And much of it on the absurd assumption that the entire regiment will somehow add increments to the individual's emotional stability and ultimate happiness. A twenty-year-old college student fires a pistol into his brain and the reaction is predictable: "Why would such a bright, promising young man do such a thing?" Had he been a high school dropout we wouldn't have been surprised, but education should, according to the myth, immunize against despondency. Some administration buildings in high schools now take on the character of a mental hygiene clinic with countless offices occupied by school psychologists, counselors, and other academic mother figures and handholders. Classes which may be in anything from home economics to biology are transformed into sensitivity sessions and group therapy hours. One teacher laid the absurdity on the line: "I don't see my role as that of teaching; I try to provide an experience in living which will help the children be happier human beings." Fine and dandy! But since, at least in name, she is a history teacher, we might hope that her pupils learn something of history. We have seen no evidence that hours and years of education in any academic environment contribute to rational, productive, or satisfying living. Learning which is applied toward the acquisition of rational goals can, indeed, lead to a more satisfying life. But the mere accumulation of facts contributes little or nothing to one's mental health. And an "education-for-the-sake-of-education" approach coupled with a liberal arts orientation designed to turn out a cocktail party acculturated, twentieth-century renaissance man, offered within the framework of classroom group psychotherapy, is unlikely to produce contented adults. Only, perhaps, confusion.

Educational Myth No. 3: Schoolteachers, counselors, and administrators have a better understanding of children and the psychological workings of your child than you do. Ever since John Dewey was canonized by the academic community, teachers have seen themselves as group psychotherapists. Freuds with blackboards. And the psychological guardians of the young. A parent-teacher conference or a welcoming talk at the school open house takes on the flavor of shop talk at a psychology convention —if psychologists talked in nothing but clichés. ("I am happy to say, Mrs. Smith, that Johnny seems to adjust well to competitive situations and is able to establish comfortable relationships with his peers, although he does seem somewhat insecure when called upon to assert his individuality and natural creativity.") Teachers who face thirty children in a classroom and have no more experience or training in diagnosing and treating psychological problems than the school custodian "authoritatively" analyze young Jimmy who has been sitting in the sixth seat, third row, for five weeks. They then advise Jimmy's parents. Of course, Jimmy's parents have been living with Jimmy for nine years, but the teacher "by reason of her training" is better able in five weeks to psych out thirty kids than their parents are. Of course, if the teacher is a bit insecure in her diagnosis, or if Jimmy is a problem in the classroom she feels she can't handle, she can send him to the counselor. The counselor or school psychologist can then approach Jimmy's poor academic performance or misbehavior on the playground as a neurosis. ("There seems to be evidence of an underlying sibling rivalry with his sister Mary, together with an attempt to compensate for his small size.") We then have the next step in the program of "school as a mental hygiene clinic." Thanks to schoolteachers speaking of all behavior in school in psychological jargon, we have parents who look at their children as if they have psyches as fragile as venetian blown glass: Don't make a move without consulting teacher; you may fracture him with complexes. Even if we were to grant the assumption that the teacher is more an authority on child-rearing practices, an assumption which hardly seems warranted by what we see in the families of teachers as well as what we observe in classrooms, we would still ask, "Do we want the teacher as an amateur psychoanalyst or as a teacher?"

Some teachers, we readily admit, may have more insight into a particular child's problems than his parents do. But then, since some parents are almost totally lacking in rationality and responsibility, a streetcar conductor might be better able to understand their child. This is certainly not reason for assuming that the teacher, by reason of her experience in teaching, is an expert in the psychological workings of all children. Nor that the teacher can understand Jimmy better than Jimmy's mother and father who are average, conscientious parents. The danger of this myth stems from the fact that parents who have accepted the teacher as psychological authority have not only turned over a major authority in the direction of child rearing, they have been intimidated into non-action. There is a very real fear on the part of many parents that they will do the "wrong" thing, i.e., psychologically damaging, if they take action on their own without first seeking the advice of the teacher or if they ignore the teacher's advice. No parent has all the answers and no parent can be totally observant or totally objective. If the teacher has picked up something in watching Jimmy, his concerned parents would want to know. The teacher, however, holds no golden key to objectivity either. Furthermore, the teacher has perhaps twenty, thirty, or more children to observe and in a much more limited environment. A teacher should be something of an authority on teaching, but neither by training nor experience in a classroom is the teacher an authority on either child psychology or child rearing.

Educational Myth No. 4: The teaching method employed is most important to the outcome of the child's education. Teaching school, like any other job, has its boring hours. As any parent knows, one can grow weary talking to "little people" hours on end. Perhaps this has something to do with why teachers are so quick to introduce the latest educational fad, gimmick, and method; it relieves boredom—the teacher's boredom. But does it make much real difference in how much the children learn? Who knows? If the schools had to test out the programs and establish their effectiveness before they introduced them, usually at incredible expense, they might have to keep teaching in the same way and all the excitement of a new fad would be lost. So the programs are seldom tested; they are wrapped in an attractive package of pedagogical rhetoric and bright new books, tapes, films, and assorted A-V aids and sold to the parents. Fads in teaching methods and materials are matched by fads in teaching "philosophies." Every year another book or two comes out proposing a new "analysis" of the child and how he learns. Usually it is written by a former schoolteacher who then tours the country, talking to educators, and signing autographed copies. The teachers react as if they had discovered the Holy Grail. The book will be talked about at conferences of teachers and they will vie with one another in their attempts to adopt the new book to the classroom. To be old-fashioned in teaching is to commit all the seven deadly sins at once. The adaptations supposedly based on the "new philosophy" generally fly off in all directions. They thus serve the purpose of further confusing most parents and children. And almost never do they contribute to more efficient learning or more effective teaching. A good teacher knows the subject matter, is able to organize it, and get it across, and no "new approach" will turn a poor teacher into a good one.

Parents as well as teachers can be caught up in the search for an educational "magic key." In recent years, it has been the parents who have bought the books on educational theory and it has been the parents, every bit as much as the teachers, who have pushed for the latest educational innovation. This has led to the establishment of whole institutions in the form of private schools which promise wonders in the education of the child through faith in the new philosophy. Several years ago, the Montessori method caught on (actually, it had been around for many decades). More recently, the Summerhill approach flared the imagination of parents. These "new" approaches to education have an understandable appeal: They always sound as if the "final cure" has been discovered. Furthermore, the cure will be painless. The fads come and they go as parents discover the fad is not producing a miracle. It never will.

Educational Myth No. 5: An understanding teacher who can establish good rapport with the students is the best teacher. Best for what? The theory—and it is only a theory—is to the effect that the teacher who can attract students is the teacher capable of "relating" to them and who can therefore inspire them to learn. It's an attractive theory, and who would argue that the lovable teacher makes the hours in the classroom more pleasant, but does "rapport" (another overused psychological term) contribute to learning? If any of us with a dozen or more years' educational experience think back over that experience, chances are we will recall teachers we learned much from but with whom we had very poor rapport, teachers who may have literally scared the wits out of us.

There are scores of teachers who seem to be continually competing for the title "Most Popular Teacher." Today, that may translate "the teacher who most often sides with the students against the establishment and the parents" and/or "the teacher who makes the fewest demands on the students" and/or "the teacher who tries to be 'with it,' who identifies with the kids' opinions and fads." Such teachers may win the contest, but no prize as teachers. The price of popularity through becoming an easygoing, permissive, nice guy is paid in teaching effectiveness when teachers fail to make the demands which are necessary and fail to assert the authority which is essential. Ironically, children usually see through it. They can spot the teacher who is trying to be the popular, nice guy and they quickly learn to use it to their advantage. Unfortunately, the advantage is not educational. Somehow, the students seem to know why they're there even if the teachers don't. The students recognize that they are there to learn and they respect the teacher who respects their ability to learn and who demands that they develop their capabilities. Certainly we are not saying that the tyrannical teacher is the best teacher. We are saying, however, that popularity and good rapport are not the primary qualifications of a good teacher. The first question should not be "Do the students like Mrs. So and So?" but "Do the students learn from Mrs. So and So?"

Educational Myth No. 6: Parents can best further their children's education by cooperating closely with the school. This one reverses the order of things. Parents have the responsibility for the education of their children. They can delegate some teaching functions to schoolteachers and others, but they cannot hand over the responsibility; it is theirs. We might never know it, however, from the propagandizing this myth gets. From the first PTA meeting of the year through each parent-teacher conference, parents are asked, then thanked for, their cooperation. It all sounds sensible and reasonable enough, but it is based on an underlying assumption which should be seriously questioned. "That the school holds the primary responsibility for the child's education and that you, as a 'good parent,' must follow the prescriptions and suggestions of the teachers: Teacher knows best."

But *does* teacher know best? The teacher has an opinion on what he or she feels the child should learn. So does the parent. If the opinions differ, can anyone argue rationally that the responsibility of the teacher stands above that of the parent and that the teacher's opinion should, therefore, prevail? Teachers, of course, don't claim they have the primary responsibility. At least they say they don't. But as every parent who has sat through the pedantics of a parent-teacher conference knows, the issue is not a straw man. Teachers, youth leaders, and other self-appointed experts, and even neighbors have assumed a responsibility and an authority which should remain with the parents. In fairness to the teachers, it must be said that when they argue that the schools have been forced to step in and assume responsibilities where the parents have not done so, they are not entirely wrong. More than a few parents have copped out in almost all areas of child rearing, including education. Parents have asked the schools to take over the discipline of their children (while not permitting them to punish them), to teach them about sex, drugs, and sewing, to instruct them in religion, morals, and the motor vehicle laws, and to impose dress standards, curfews, and courtesies. No one can fault the teachers for asking, "If the parents don't do it, and we won't do it, who will?" The sad truth of the matter, however, is that if the parents refuse to assume the responsibility, no attempt on the part of the schools is probably going to be effective. Lack of responsibility on the part of some parents hardly seems to be the issue. What of the large number of rational, concerned parents who have not resigned their parenthood? Are the teachers willing to recognize this and leave the primary responsibility to them? Don't bet on it. It is likely to become a power struggle to determine who is to cooperate with whom. Teachers are not only convinced they know best for your child; they are sure you are trying to subvert the system and destroy your child if you don't fall in line behind their views and back them up in all things. "Never let your child think you believe the teacher is wrong" is the first pedagogical commandment. Teachers *are*, nevertheless, human beings who come in all sizes and shapes, intellectually as well as physically, and they *can* be wrong. They can be mistaken in their facts and confused in their values every bit as much as their pupils' parents. We send the child to school hoping that he or she will learn what is true and valid and to be taught that which makes sense. Frequently, the child will check out with his parents material presented by the teacher. If the parent persistently agrees with and backs up the teacher when the teacher is in error or is teaching what is irrational, the child may, in time, reach an age when he or she decides everything and everyone in the establishment is either stupid or crazy.

By any reasoning, the schools should be attempting to cooperate with the parents in working toward the goals which the parents, assuming their responsibility, set forth. This has its obvious practical limitations when we are speaking of a large number of families with perhaps very divergent goals. The principle, however, should not be abandoned. Within the framework of what the schools have to offer, it is up to the parents to decide what is best for their child and it is their responsibility to make this known to the teacher.

There is another myth which pervades just about everything in our schools today. It is more than a myth, it is a philosophical cornerstone. In effect it says, "All children are created equal and we must do everything possible to ensure that they remain equal." If the college football coach conducted training on the same philosophy, he would encourage his giant linebacker to slim down to 150 pounds to "even things out" when the team is scheduled to meet a lighter opponent. He would bar his star quarterback from practice in order to ensure that the star would not get too far ahead of the others.

Not only is this philosophy responsible for the "no failure" approach, it underlies the course content and academic demands from first grade through high school (and it is spreading fungus-like into the colleges). The thinking goes something like this: "If we reduce the courses to mediocrity, then everyone will be able to keep up with the class, no one will feel left out, no one will fail, and everyone will feel that he is equal. Ignore the fact that Willie has an IQ of 89 while Betsy, sitting across the aisle, has an IQ of 135. Pretend that the fact that Kenneth's parents are highly educated adults who read a great deal and place strong emphasis on education while Kevin's parents spend most of their leisure hours drinking beer in front of a television set and have no interest in their children's education is of no significance. We may not like facing realities, but shutting our eyes to them will not make them go away. Human beings are *not* equally endowed intellectually or physically. If they were, we could all make a choice of being an Albert Einstein or a Willie Mays. Ignoring individual differences not only penalizes the bright student and deceives the not-so-bright, it leaves all students ill prepared for the adult world they will someday enter. The bright student will not have been given enough; the dull student will be handed a diploma which is meaningless. This is a dishonest game no matter how you look at it. It may seem charitable to wrap children in a psychological cotton batting, but the days of reckoning and reality have a way of coming. The adult world is a competitive world, one in which individual differences show up very dramatically and are either rewarded or punished in terms of achievement, status, and contribution. To create an environment in a school which shields the child as long as possible from any recognition of this reality is to set the child up for a mighty fall. No one would suggest that a child be taught to view himself as a failure. But it is equally harmful to teach him unrealistically that he is a success. Children have a way of discovering the lies of adults. We may set up ungraded classes, but children know which students are the brightest and which students have difficulty grasping the material, and all the artificial structuring the schools may attempt will not keep the secret from them. All children should have an equal chance to pursue an education. To treat children as if they are all equal in their capabilities in taking advantage of the education offered is, however, not an exercise in "fairness," only a dreadful falsehood.

Taking the Parental Reins. Trying to "fight City Hall" is always a frustration. Fighting the applied mythology of the schools is even more vexing, as many parents have discovered. Anyone who has sat through a meeting of a Board of Education knows what an avalanche of rhetoric can be loosed to bury probing questions. Parent-teacher conferences can be almost as bad.

We have talked to many parents who have expressed

more than mild dissatisfaction with their children's schools, but who have felt powerless to combat the irrationalities. Following the old rule of thumb which says, "If you can't fight 'em, join 'em," they have all but surrendered to the educators. Can they do anything else? Is there much, if any, hope that the rational concerned parent can win against the educational City Hall? *Yes* and *No*. Parents might try to get on the inside and work to change the system, become active in PTA and home-school groups, and endeavor to influence the direction of the schools. They might run for a seat on the school board or back candidates for the board who promise to work for the changes they can support. It's possible that their efforts might pay off, but if we may be forgiven our cynicism, we don't hold out much hope. As every *candid* teacher and school principal will admit, PTA members often unwittingly serve the causes of the school, not the child. They are in the vanguard working to pass school bonds; they raise money to purchase movie projectors for the classrooms; they volunteer to serve as room mothers. But generally, PTA meetings are as non-controversial as a Mother's Day editorial. And as little concerned with academic programming. The administrators and teachers are the experts. They let the parents know what they have already decided they are going to give to, and do to, the children left in their charge. The roles are so well entrenched that the parent with the temerity to challenge the program is likely to find other parents forming into a protection phalanx around the teachers. Anything less than unquestioning acceptance is apt to be viewed as a personal attack on the academic papacy. Reactions at most school-board meetings are seldom anything other than docile (unless the issue is money). We all would like to believe in the power of the voice of people, but when the people's voice becomes a mere echo of the mythology, then perhaps we have to accept what can and cannot be changed. Changing the system may not be possible, but much *can* be done to give your child the education you want for him—with or without much help from those within the system.

1. *Keep in mind you are the expert.* You can listen to the opinions of other parents, teachers, and your children; but when all is said and done, we, the parents, have the responsibility of deciding what we want our children to learn and how to ensure that they are able to do so. We may not be able to exercise control over what goes on in their classrooms, but we can exercise control over what goes on elsewhere.

We happen to believe, for example, that a wide exposure to books—fiction and non-fiction—is important. We also feel our children do not receive enough reading in school. The amount of required reading is far less than the amount of reading we want them to do. Our answer has been a family reading program. In addition to our own fairly extensive library (mostly paperbacks and a bit of everything), there is the nearby public library. Once each week or two, we have a family trip to the library. The children can each make one "free choice"—a book of their own choosing, fiction or non-fiction—and we select a book, or sometimes two, for each child. They are held responsible for the required reading which becomes a topic for informal discussion, often during the evening meal. By selecting the required books, we can ensure a somewhat balanced reading diet. We have found it takes some imagination, but similar programs, formal or informal, can be initiated in science, art, music, or any of a number of educational areas. To be sure, there is a demand made on the parental time, and time, for most of us, is always at a premium. These programs can, however, be not only enriching, but enjoyable to both the parents and the children. They may even provide genuine opportunities to make learning *fun*. We have found that a lot of what we think of as family entertainment today began as an "educational program." In considering such home-based programs, we are always faced with the alternative: To leave it to the schools and hope we can be satisfied with what they are providing.

There may be times, especially in the beginning, when you run into opposition. If one of the children doesn't care for reading (and that's generally the child most in need of it), he may argue that it isn't fair to demand more than the teachers demand. Teachers and friends may tell you you're placing too much pressure on your children. Remember, however, you have the ultimate responsibility and you are the *expert*.

2. *Learn to use the teacher as a source of information.* If you want to know what your child is doing in school, you can find out a lot from your child—assuming he is candid and communication is good—but you also need a line to the teachers, a line which will provide some clear-cut answers. Some contacts with teachers will prove informative; some will not.

The report card is least informative. At best, it is somewhat like a fever thermometer. You can read the thermometer to discover the patient has a temperature of 102°, but the thermometer doesn't indicate what may be causing the fever. The report card shows the teacher gave Willie a C— in history, nothing more. It doesn't say whether Willie was doing well at the start and lost his motivation, had a slow start but has been catching up lately, has had trouble understanding, has spent his time in class daydreaming, or has missed the last two weeks of school. To rely, then, on a report card to tell you much of anything of how your child may be doing in the classroom is a reliance on only the scantiest of information. Furthermore, if he has been having trouble, report cards will tell you not only too little, but too late. If you are going to provide any degree of guidance and supervision, you will need more immediate and more extensive information.

The once- or twice-a-year open house isn't much more informative. Generally, it follows a standard format. The principal gives a short welcoming speech and the parents are then directed to their children's classrooms where they can search out their offsprings' drawing among the others tacked around the room. The teacher may give a short explanation of the exciting things planned for the school year, and at the conclusion the parents may vie with each other for a short private audience with the teacher. If they succeed, they are told what a delight it is to have Willie or Johnny or Betsy in the class. After cookies, coffee, and punch, the parents leave knowing no more than they did when they came.

The one-to-one parent-teacher conference, on the other hand, may be very informative, but only if the parent goes in with a plan. Without a plan, the conference can be a waste of time for both parent and teacher. Usually the teacher will string together the standard school euphemisms: "Willie is such an active boy"—translation: "I'd like to be able to nail your kid to his seat." "Betsy always has such interesting stories to tell"—translation: "You'd never believe what Betsy told us of what goes on in your home." "Johnny shows a natural leadership ability"—translation: "Your son's gang is terrorizing the playground." Even with the knowledge of the code the parent may not learn much. The teacher may report that Johnny is doing "just fine" in everything. The report, however, doesn't tell what is being offered in the classroom or what criteria the teacher uses for just fine. Johnny's teacher may be satisfied with average work. Johnny's parents, on the other hand, knowing Johnny is bright and capable of doing much better, may expect a good deal more of him. The teacher may run a permissive class in which she is willing to accept as "normal" certain behavior which the parents would never permit. You can usually dig out the information you are looking for if you walk into the conference with specific, well-planned questions. If circumstances cannot permit both of us parents to attend a conference, we may have a briefing session a day or two ahead so that we can share observations and formulate questions. The questions may grow out of the day-to-day conversations with the child. (Soon after he has arrived home from school—while it is fresh—is a good time to hear about his day at school.) Questions can also be raised from examination of the work papers he has brought home. We require that all assignment papers, tests, etc., which are returned by the teacher, be brought home. There may also be some stock questions. These can be open-ended questions such as "Which subjects seem to cause him the most trouble?" "Are there materials I can help him with at home?" "What can you tell me about his playmates?" "How is his behavior in class?"—"on the playground?" "Does he get his work in on time?"

The important thing to remember is that you—the parent and expert—are seeking information which you can then assess and use in planning an educational program for your child. The teacher will, no doubt, have opinions on what you should expect and demand as well as what goals you should set in his education. But while you may, and should, consider the opinions carefully, they should never be treated as dogma, they're merely the opinions of one other adult.

Approaching the parent-teacher conference with the goal of information gathering, you may find some interesting reactions from the teacher. The teacher may be unsettled by the relatively rare experience of encountering parents who are genuinely interested in what their child is doing in school. They are accustomed to dealing with parents who prefer leaving education firmly in the lap of the school; parents who go through such conferences as a mere ritual, or as a gripe session. Once the initial shock has worn off, the parents and teacher can get down to the business of discussing the child. It is here that diplomacy is called for. You want all the information you can get. More information than the teacher is accustomed to providing. This means enticing the teacher over to your side. Without cooperation from the teacher above and beyond what is generally offered, the conference will provide little you can employ. If the teacher begins to feel under attack, a defensive game may ensue and you will be stymied. Worse yet, you could end up with the teacher as an enemy. If that happens, your child may be the loser. You may be able to increase the amount of information you can garner from the conference if both of you, Father *and* Mother, attend the conference. The conferences are usually scheduled during the day when most fathers are working, but if Dad can take off from work it may prove to be worthwhile. Teachers are accustomed to dealing with mothers and perhaps they are thrown somewhat off balance when confronted with a father; but for whatever reasons, we have observed that fathers can go further in clarifying things with teachers than mothers can alone—especially if Dad is willing to assume authority during the meeting. If what you want for your child is going to necessitate battling it out with administrators, it would be especially important to be able to present a united front through the presence of both parents. There are times when a little extra "muscle" is needed.

3. *Establish your criteria for acceptable school performance and a home program necessary to maintain it.* If you were to take a random sample of a half-dozen or more children, you might have one or two who, for reasons probably never to be understood, are seemingly turned on to school achievement from kindergarten on, children who never have to be prodded to do homework assignments or study and who go along from one grade to the next operating close to capacity. But the odds on having all the children in the family such "self-starters" are not consoling to busy parents. The popular notion that if left on his own the child will become turned on to school (given, of course, a stimulating, creative teacher) and will devour everything the educational institution has to offer is the furthest departure from reality, somewhat like suggesting that if a man is happy with his vocational choice, he will go off cheerily to work each morning and never, never use his sick leave to pamper a hangover. Until they reach the age of maturity in which the goals of

education become their own goals, most children need some motivation supplied by their parents. And sermons which start, "If you're going to get into college—or get a good job—someday, you'd better develop good study habits now" are next to worthless. The sermons may make sense to the parents, but mean nothing to a twelve-year-old.

Ensuring that Johnny *works*, that is studies, to the level of his capacity, takes a few quarts of blood and sweat—from the parents. It demands *supervision*. Much more than most parents recognize. And certainly more than the permissive don't-make-demands-on-the-child teachers would condone. It also takes the perseverance and authority of a Marine drill sergeant. A parent may not want to pay the price. Many don't. That would depend on the value they place on their child's education. But as tempting as it might be, no parent should indulge in the wishful thinking that the school will provide motivation and supervision or that Johnny will be self-motivated at all times. The following are some steps we have found effective:

A. *Establish where the homework and studying are to be done*. The child's room is probably the least desirable. You may keep him out from underfoot, but that's about all. Not only is it filled with distractions, it makes supervision virtually impossible. He goes off to his room to "study" and two hours later reports all the homework done. You have no way of being sure he was reading history instead of comics. That desk you bought for his room isn't likely to provide a magical stimulus for study. And lying on his bed with a history book is a good way to fall asleep.

Since the after-school hours are usually spent by Mother in the kitchen, the kitchen table probably provides the best place for supervised homework. Mother can continue with her preparations for dinner while keeping one eye on the schoolwork. There is an added advantage in being able to have the children in a centralized study area. Since the table is usually large enough to accommodate all of them, it will eliminate the problem of running back and forth to check on them.

If the children have been in the habit of studying in their room, stand by for a blow the first time you attempt to move them to the kitchen table. After all, what child likes that degree of supervision? Like it or not, however, once they discover the rule is going to stand, they will, hopefully, relax their resistance. (We did say *hopefully*.) Supervision, in this case, means *supervision*. To be effective, it must be active, not passive. The supervising parent will probably have to keep at least one eye on what is going on at the study table at all times to curb tendencies to daydream, chat, or in other ways goof off. The boom may have to be lowered to remind a wandering student of why he or she is there. One thing to remember: You can't simply start the operation and expect it to run as a perpetual motion machine. The supervision must be consistent if it is to be effective. Of course, there is nothing to prevent the parents from spelling each other when both are at home, so Dad may take over the supervisory task when he arrives from work.

Although such tight supervision may sound somewhat like a job for a prison guard, it isn't really much different from what a good teacher does in a classroom. The parents merely establish a second classroom in the home. Classroom notes are checked, assignments are gone over, projects are discussed, and additional work such as arithmetic exercises when needed is assigned. How many years does this go on? That depends. Somewhere along the line, the child may begin reaping some rewards for his scholastic endeavor in terms of grades, praise from teachers, and the achievement of being top in the class. The rewards may then act as a positive motivation to turn him on academically. When this has become consistent, you may be able to slack off on "cracking the whip" but speaking realistically, the supervision cannot be wholly abandoned until high school is completed. A child can turn off as well as turn on, and the child who worked for top grades in seventh grade may quit entirely in the eighth grade.

The question of how much time is to be spent in homework and study will, of course, be answered in terms of grade in school, amount of outside work assigned by the teacher, and how well you feel the child is doing academically. Chances are, however, the amount of outside homework and study necessary to achieve what you have determined he is capable of achieving will be more than he will attempt to convince you is necessary. And speaking strictly in terms of homework assignment time, he well may be right since the demands of most teachers are far from stringent. But remember, *you* set the criteria. A couple of retorts to look out for: "I did my homework in study hall," and "My teacher never assigns homework." Study halls, whatever their purpose, are not environments for study. It is possible some studying might be done, but far from probable. Study hall may be recommended by his counselor, but don't expect a rational answer when you ask, "Why?" Unless the child is working at least a half-time job or milking at least forty cows every afternoon after school, he has more than enough time to complete all homework and studying at home. More important, if he is permitted to take a study hall, and supposedly does his homework during study hall (and in high school, one hour will almost never be sufficient), you have lost your supervision; as with studying in his room, he tells you that the work has been completed in study hall and you have no way of knowing whether he is, in fact, doing much of anything—at least until the report card comes home.

It is true that teachers differ in their emphasis on homework, and some have strong convictions against "imposing" any outside assignments on their students. Some don't want to put too much "pressure" on the child; others argue that the child needs recreational time, and perhaps if they were candid, some teachers might admit correcting homework assignments adds more work to their jobs. The only way you may be able to be certain is by checking with the teacher, and by the time your child reaches high school, or even junior high, this may be an involved business. Today, in many of our larger high schools, it is easier to complete a phone call to Howard Hughes than to get through to your children's teachers. Any contact must be made through the counselor or adviser and often the feedback from the teacher—via the counselor—is no more informative than a report card. If you are insistent, however, you just may be able to get through and discover exactly what is or is not expected by way of homework assignments—even if you have to go to the school and catch the teacher outside the classroom after school —and hope you're not arrested for trespassing.

A distinction should be made. We have used two words: *homework* and *studying*. They are not necessarily synonymous. Johnny may report that his homework for the day is completed and it may be. But sitting down with his history book, studying the material, taking notes on it, may not be, in Johnny's estimation, under the heading of *homework*. In most subjects, both homework assignments *and* studying are called for. Furthermore, Johnny isn't apt to skip through the homework in a slapdash fashion to escape from the study table if he knows that the answer will be "Fine, now you can get some good time in studying your history."

B. *Check the schoolwork.* The ground rule we have found to be effective: All books and schoolwork are to be brought home *each day.* In grammar school, the children may not have many books checked out to them; in junior high and high school, bringing all the books home which have been assigned may be quite an armful. Some of the texts may not be necessary each day, but if, on any particular day, you want to check on your child's math assignments and he has left his math book and assignments in his locker at school, you are stymied. If the assignment sheets and notebooks are brought home each day, a check can be made on what work he is doing in the classroom. Going over the notes he takes in class can be very revealing. If the "notes" consist primarily of doodling and superficial jottings, further check and some "tightening up" may be called for.

Many junior high and high school teachers hand out mimeographed assignment sheets, which make it easy to keep up with what is called for. Our blessings on such teachers. When such assignment sheets are not distributed, the child should be pressed to keep his own assignment sheet. It then becomes a simple matter to check off the assignments against the work completed.

In grammar school, checking the assignments includes checking for completion and for accuracy. High school is something else. Unless you have a knowledge of everything from French verbs to trigonometry, you won't be able to check on much more than whether he has the work completed (at least as far as you can tell). But you can check at least that much. The important point to remember is that a check be kept on what *is* being done on the homework, projects, book reports, and study. Just knowing that his work is being checked daily may prove to be a strong motivator.

C. *Set a schedule for the homework and studying.* If the homework is left pretty much on a "when-I-get-around-to-it" basis, there is a good chance it won't be done. At least it won't be done consistently. It is the pattern in most families that the homework is tackled in the evening after dinner, and obviously there is no one *best* time for all. It will probably depend on the amount of homework to be done, other assigned chores, the age of the child, and other very practical considerations. With our younger children, we have found the evening hours are poor. By that time they are tiring and alertness is waning. With our high schoolers, on the other hand, evening study hours are often a necessity; the work simply cannot always be completed in the afternoon. Television watching for our teen-agers is, therefore, usually limited to weekends (with some occasional special exceptions). We allow a flexibility based on one broad general rule: How much study time is required (and this includes *study* as well as homework assignments) and the structure in time, place, etc. we impose will be primarily influenced—if not *determined*—by how well the individual child is performing in his schoolwork (taking ability into consideration). If the last two or three report cards have been all A's we will permit considerable latitude. (But, as we might expect, the straight A student generally keeps to the same schedule without need for "enforcement.")

D. *Select the electives.* In junior high and high school, children are asked to make choices they are often unprepared to make. We have sat through the program planning sessions with entering freshmen, our own, in which the counselor has asked the stock question "What do you plan to major in in college?" and we have been tempted to come back with "What did you think you wanted to do in college when *you* were fourteen years old?" How much does the high school student know what will prepare him for college, or what career he may choose two, three, or even ten years later? In the ninth grade, Johnny may live for nothing but hot rods and dream of little except the day he may own one of his own. He tells the counselor he wants to be an automotive mechanic and the counselor directs him into mechanical drawing and shop courses. No math. No languages. And no science beyond the one or two basic courses. But Johnny's interests don't stand still. By eighteen, he may have started thinking of a career in medicine. Now comes the rude awakening. He can't meet the requirements of the colleges he might select. The sad irony lies in the fact that he has probably spent four years tinkering around in playroom shop courses which will not equip him to be the mechanic

he originally planned to be! High schools and even junior
high schools are cluttered with non-academic courses more
suited to Disneyland which serve a baby-sitting function
(at incredible expense) for the unmotivated. Supposedly,
they provide a little something for everybody and round
out the curriculum. In reality, they provide little or nothing for *anybody,* other than recreation and a chance to
goof off one hour a day. Shop courses generally fall into
this category—along with *television arts, senior problems*
(a daily rap session), *yearbook* (for credit), *journalism,
office monitor, audio visual monitor, motion picture viewing* (for English credit yet). Not all students, of course,
are capable of successfully completing a "straight academic" program and it would be unfair to them and to
the other students to require them to enroll in geometry
and physics. For them, shop courses might be the answers,
yet one might wonder why the shop courses so seldom
offer much solid vocational preparation. To permit the
academically capable student to enroll in such tempting
fun courses is a disservice. Some counselors may try to
talk the student out of signing up for a shop course, but
given a persistent student, few counselors will hold a hard
line. This is where parents take over.

The program should be gone over by parent and child
each year and approved by the *parent.* If the child is intellectually equipped to go beyond high school he should
be academically prepared to do so. He may decide after
graduation that college is not for him, but at least he
should be prepared by his course work to *make* such a
choice. Catalogues and some of the paperback books and
magazine articles on admission to college may give parents the necessary guide to requirements; the school
counselor may also be able to provide information which
will help in planning the program. Just don't rely on the
counselor to do the planning. It is not his responsibility.
It is the parents'. Parental responsibility also calls for active involvement on a day-by-day basis, but within cau-
tious limits.

Offer help, but don't do it for them. This is a tough one. Once you get a hand into the homework, it is often tempting to go too far in showing children "how to do it." Since it is easier to do it yourself than painstakingly to work to teach your child, frustration may prevail and you may end up taking over. Remember, however, that in any help you give in the homework you are a *teacher*, not a demonstrator and not the student. Once you have shown him how to do it, let him take over and carry on from there. With arithmetic, for example, if he is stuck on long division, it does no good to show him how to do the problems by doing some of the assigned problems as "examples." That merely lets him out of some of the homework and he is learning nothing. Make up some examples of your own, work them to show him how, then let him work the assignments on his own. Kids can be great con artists, as every parent knows. If Johnny can get his parents to do the homework for him, he wins at the con game. But Johnny doesn't learn much from it except how to con his parents. Your involvement in the homework should be primarily to supervise; secondarily, to teach. Any help given should be the minimum amount necessary in order to enable the child to do it on his own. If you carry it too far, he may develop far too much dependence. It would be better, perhaps, to allow him to make mistakes which you can catch when you check the homework. He may not enjoy having to go back and redo the work, but the learning may be worth it.

What about those projects so dear to the hearts of teachers? A few years ago, a sixth-grade teacher of one of our daughters assigned a project to each student to construct a miniature parade float representing one of the fifty states or U.S. territories. Our daughter attacked the project with enthusiasm, and after much planning and hard work, she produced a very imaginative float representing the state of Iowa, cornstalks and all. In our eyes (admittedly biased) it was a superior job. It did not, however, get her an A from the teacher. One float which did draw an A, was a scale model of the Lincoln Memorial representing the District of Columbia. It was done all in sugar cubes! Another A float was a plaster and papier-mâché model of the state of Texas complete with working oil pumps! By sixth graders? Who is kidding whom? Projects are assigned by teachers, done by parents, and a grade given to the child. Needless to say, no one admits to the deception. Who knows? They might not even recognize the dishonesty involved. Perhaps only the child sees it for what it truly is. This "help" from parents, which becomes a take-over and results in parents vying with other parents for school grades and prizes, puts the child on the spot. He knows he didn't do the work and he suspects the teacher and the other children also know it. (And they do.) Yet he has to play out the deception for the sake of his competitive parents and a teacher who is willing to shut her eyes to a child's ethical dilemma. No one set of parents will probably be able to influence all other parents or teachers to stop this destructive business but they can at least make it known to their children that they are aware of what these adults are doing and they can encourage their children to achieve on their own merits—and praise them when they do. The praise may not wipe out the sting of injustice when classmates win prizes for projects executed by their parents in conspiracy with teachers, but at least the child will know his parents maintain some degree of integrity and that they value his worth and his capabilities.

Today, many of the young talk of a need to fight the "establishment" or the "system," and a dismaying minority have turned their words into action. Perhaps it is the parents who must fight the system for the control of the education and guidance of their children. In a day in which teachers and administrators encourage mediocrity and strive to make Orwellian adjustment the highest goal of the schools, our courts further split the family and the neighborhood by bussing children in the name of racial balance, and children are taught they have rights rather than responsibilities, what choices do we have? If we, their parents, do not fight for the survival of our children, we will be guilty of delivering them up to the brainwashers and brain destroyers of a malignant system.

8

THE SCENE TODAY:
DOING THEIR OWN THING

"Kids are kids; they're no different today from what they were in our day" is a view no parent can afford to hold. If children are not different, their world certainly is, and they are affected by that world. Parents can make no more serious mistake than to ignore this. Each time we have talked to a group of parents we have heard from someone that all this concern with the younger generation is unwarranted, that they also did a lot of "dumb kid stunts" when they were the same age. As strongly as we can, we point out the error in such thinking. It simply is *not* the same. When we were twelve, we tried cigarettes. And maybe we were caught and punished. Now, twelve-year-olds are swallowing barbiturates and pep pills. At fourteen, we played post office and spin-the-bottle. Today, fourteen-year-olds are being treated for venereal disease. We may have done our share of vandalism and pranks; we may even have gained some reputation for wildness. No one speaks of wildness today. It just doesn't seem to fit the behavior of a group of students who burn a high school, a teenage shoplifting gang, or boys and girls who beat up a policeman during a demonstration.

The comparison breaks down in many other areas as well. Our world of childhood was relatively simple. We knew what we believed in (usually, it followed what our parents believed in), what we were working toward (the Great American Dream), and what means we could and could not employ to reach these goals. We knew parents and teachers had rights. It never occurred to us that we had any. We may have resented the exercise of their authority, but we would not have dared rebel against it. The world was changing then, but the changes, we felt sure, were all for the better, all in the name of progress. Our life would be a better life than our parents'; they told us it would be. Morality and ethics were black and white. The good guys wore the white hats. And Horatio Alger was alive and well and living in the hearts of youth and the aspirations of their parents.

We listened to radio and scanned newspapers and magazines (but not much). Even younger parents today were not raised on television in the way their children are. Twenty years ago, television viewing meant quiz shows, wrestling, and Uncle Miltie. Television news was mostly wire service copy read in an unimaginative style by a man seated behind a desk, hardly designed to attract children (or many adults). Today, TV viewing accounts for more than six hours of each day in the average American home. Our children are not the Spock generation, nor the drug generation, nor even the love generation. But without question, they are the TV generation. News, through the wonders of television, is no longer merely news; it is entertainment. Lying on the floor before the set, our children can watch riots, wars, murders, strikes, starvation, Olympic competition, polluted atmosphere, moon walks, underwater explorations, visits to ghettos and palaces, political intrigues and heart transplants. All in living color.

Scores of articles have been written on the effects of television on children. (Surprisingly few people seem concerned with its effects on adults.) With a few notable exceptions, the articles have been grounded more in polemics than sober research. And they seem to have had little noticeable effect on either viewing habits or programing.

We all seem to agree children are better informed today as a result of television, but we seldom question whether TV is presenting reality. Even those in the industry will admit that it is not, and that it cannot. Television presents an edited picture of an attenuated society, selected for dramatic interest. This isn't an indictment of the industry, only a recognition of the scope and limitations of the medium. A news story covering the events of perhaps twenty-four hours with background events spanning months or even years edited to a five-minute news spot—or even an hour long "special"—can only distort reality, regardless of the honesty and objectivity of those responsible for its production. From their earliest years, children are bombarded with television sights and sounds. And they react to them. With the sights and sounds reflecting only a piece of a larger reality, the reactions will be marked by an equal lack of dimension.

Children today are told they should become "involved." It is the word of today, standing with "encounter" and "meaningful." Their parents' generation was given no such message. Grownups, we were told, knew best and our involvement was neither invited nor accepted. Today, the President of the United States calls a White House Conference on Youth in which representatives of youth are invited to prepare position papers on education, race relations, foreign policy, and a variety of other vital issues. These young people are well informed, at least to the extent they can be through our mass media, particularly television. Adults have recognized this and have been awed by it, so much so they have frequently shut their eyes to the obvious limitations of youth: questionable sound judgment owing to a lack of broadly based experience.

In giving youth the status they now enjoy, we have done them no favor. We have deceived children into believing that sixteen years of living in the very limited environments of home and school with little responsibility demanded are sufficient experience and knowledge to cope with and solve all the world's ills. Is it any wonder children are turning to some very maladaptive life styles in their attempts to meet these challenges? How often they have been told—by adults—their parents and teachers have no answers, that the older generation must look to them. In the face of such adult abdication of both responsibility and intellect, should we be surprised that so many children are saying, "Don't trust anyone over thirty."

Rapid changes in the technology bring with them changes in the entire fabric of a society. In the upheaval of the Industrial Revolution, the social institutions of the time were shaken to their foundations. The past twenty-five years have seen changes in the technology even more dramatic and significant than those of the Industrial Revolution. Following in the wake of these changes, nearly all our existing institutions are being brought into question: religion, schools and colleges, marriage, the economy, and government. The questions should be asked. The relevancy of our institutions should be reassessed. Some of them, perhaps all, will undergo radical changes or simply cease to exist. In the fifties and sixties, the questioning often led to an intellectual and moral retreat. On all sides, adults have attacked the existing institutions or deserted them and called for their downfall. They found their church no longer relevant, and they rejected it. They judged the schools no longer served the needs of the society and should tumble. The government was no longer responsive, and they muttered of rebellion.

Not all, of course. There were those who tried to ignore the changes and their implications. They became the defenders of the status quo, often as militant as the rebels. They proposed, with vigor, yesterday's solutions to the problems of today. They may not have lacked moral strength, but they frequently revealed a bareness of intellect and foresight.

The young heard the voices on both sides and rejected both. The iconoclasts who cried of the failures of our institutions yet offered no remedies were given the youthful contempt they deserved. The reactionaries preaching a "return to the good old days" found themselves dismissed with ridicule. The liberals among the parents, teachers, ministers, and politicians embraced a psychology of self-doubt which grew to become an orgy of self-flagellation. Adults who saw themselves as failures, impotent neo-reformationists, devoid of inner direction (and not un-realistically), turned to the most implausible anti-heroes for answers—their children. Despite the obvious, that the children were the least qualified to accept the charismatic mantle, youth assumed a leadership, perhaps by default. If the adults wouldn't lead, they would.

The entire concept of *rights* underwent transformation. In the late fifties and early sixties, the young were recruited to join in the demonstrations for racial justice. Few of us were not impressed by their understanding of the issues and their dedication to principles of equality.

Then something went wrong. *Rights* were asserted for every cause attractive to the young. No one told them that collective might does not, in itself, bestow any rights, that all the clubs and guns of Hitler's storm troopers did not give the Nazis the *right* to exterminate Jews. No one ex-plained to them that the *right* to freedom to pursue a goal is not the right to the goal itself, and certainly not the right to that goal by the infringement on the rights of others. And no one pointed out the basic maxim of law and foundation of all justice, that a *right*, any right, carries with it a correlative duty to respect the rights of others.

Now we have children claiming a *right* to select the school curriculum, the *right* to an "open campus," the *right* to declare a school regulation void, the *right* to distribute an anti-administration newspaper on the school grounds, the *right* to establish school policy, the *right* to break laws with assurance of amnesty. Recently, we spoke with a teacher who told us of a boy in her class who became un-ruly. He threw a book at her and let go with a string of four-letter-word insults. She sent him to the principal's office, but no immediate action was taken; it was not even clear there would be. Last year, the students were suc-cessful in pushing through a student's "bill of rights." One concession called for establishment of a grievance com-mittee to hear and decide cases in which the teacher has brought "charges" against a student. Half the committee members are teachers, half are students. And this is a grammar school!

The concept of *rights* has been redefined in a way that children—and a disturbing number of adults—believe an interest in any benefits bestowed carries with it an authority to dictate how the benefits are to be given, to whom, and in what amounts. By this "reasoning," the friendly waitress who is named in the old widower's will should have the *right* to dictate how much she is to inherit and the terms of the will. Since students benefit from the collective offerings of a college faculty and the facilities of the institution, the students have the "right" to burn down the college if they choose. Or to hire and fire their instructors. Or decide what courses should be offered or dropped (regardless of what the faculty might think best or the interests of a minority of students). And since they are receiving the benefit of financial support when they go off to college, they have the right to tell their parents where they intend to go to college, and how much they expect to be paid to go there. Our eldest daughter, a sixteen-year-old honor student, was graduating from high school and had made application to a nearby state college. When he heard of it, one of her teachers strongly advised against her choice. He thought she should go away to one of the more prestigious universities. She told him she was more than satisfied with the academic standing of the state college and that it was more within her means. "Well," he said, "your father can afford a private college, and it's your right to demand it." How do you suppose this teacher defines a *right*? On what are all these so-called rights based? From what are they derived? With so many adults so totally confused, so generally mixed up in their values and concepts, is it any wonder the youth of today are turning to: *Revolution.*

If we listened to some, we might believe all children are in a state of rebellion, that they are rebellious by their very nature. Schooled by these doomsayers, parents gird their psychological loins and brace themselves for tortuous years ahead as their children enter the *terrible teens*.

Now, it is no longer the terrible teens alone. It is also the rebellious preteens and the obstreperous grammar schoolers. Nine-year-olds tell off their mothers in the language of stevedores. Eleven-year-olds organize a sit-down strike in the principal's office. And a ten-year-old leads a gang extorting money from first and second graders.

But rebellion? We don't think so. And not revolution. It comes closer to being a cry for help!

The child of the seventies is expanding, often explosively, into a vacuum created by adults. His parents tell him the world is insane. Isn't it? They say madmen are pushing buttons which control us all, which keep in motion the endless treadmills on which we run. Stop, stand still, and you may be crushed. Pause, think, and you may be overwhelmed with despair. The Ship of Fools is a slave galley; we are the slaves. A fourteen-year-old asked her father, "What is life all about?" He answered: "If I knew, I might kill myself." She swallowed a lethal number of her mother's sleeping pills.

There is another child. He listens to the intellectual and moral bankruptcy proceedings of his elders; he refuses to join in the vacuity of despair. The past and present have not yet hardened his cortical arteries and squeezed out his vitality and hope. The apathy of his elders influences him, but in him it is transmuted into rage. Still seeking answers, he asks his parents, his teachers, those ordained to guide and encourage him, "Why shouldn't I blow up this building?" And when they offer only silence and non-answers, he lights the fuse.

Children will "test the limits," push as far as they can. They want to find a game with rules they can understand. They seek what we all want: a world with structure. No one can long tolerate a state of anarchy, whether within a state or a family. The rebellious child is not a happy child. His life is one of confusion and frustration. Despite what he may say of wanting to do his "own thing" and overturn the "establishment" of parents, school, and society, he is not looking for a life without rules. He wants them, but he wants rules based on: 1. *Well-reasoned principles* which can be proven to be rational, productive. 2. *Justice,* not capriciousness. 3. *Certainty,* clearly outlining his rights, duties, and limits.

It is in providing rules which meet these criteria that the liberal non-committed adults, the cynical inconoclastic cause-for-the-sake-of-cause adults, and the rigid status quo adults have failed so miserably.

Unless the rules are based upon well-reasoned principles which can be shown to be productive, the child can be expected to reject them. He should. Children want to know the "why" behind any rule—and the why had better elicit a pragmatic answer. Here, many parents often fall down. They may profess certain principles (although many have not worked out firm values), they may defend their positions vigorously, but if they cannot present these values which will make clear how these values will benefit the individual, no child will accept them for long. Children may lack maturity; they may lack knowledge; but they are not fools. They won't buy empty principles which form a road map to nowhere. Say to a child, "I believe in—" (God, Free Enterprise, the Catholic Church, Law and Order, the Democratic Party), and you had better be able to add "because it contributes to making my life happier or more satisfying in the following ways:——." Beliefs and convictions not based on reason are superstitions, prejudices, or conditioned responses. Rules built upon them are tyrannical. They deserve the resistance they invite. The rebellion of children, whatever their age, is not so much a rebellion against rules as it is a rejection of irrational rules administered with little attention to reason, justice, or consistency.

If the child knows he can go just so far and no further and that the limits are rational and will be strictly—but justly—enforced, he can relax and live within them. But let him live with adults who set few limits on themselves, or set few limits on their children or neglect to enforce them, and he can be counted on to rebel. Parents who don't practice self-discipline don't succeed in disciplining their children.

When the hippie culture took roots in the Haight-Ashbury district of San Francisco and while the young people were still being romanticized as "flower children," we spent time there talking with them, sharing their food and drink, listening to them talk of their lives and philosophies. We read what the newspapers and the suburban pundits said of them from a distance. These children, they claimed, had left their homes and gravitated to an environment of pot, crash pads, acid, and psychedelia to escape the cruel suppression of overly strict parents. We heard the same claim from some of the children. "Man, at home they were on my back every minute. I could never do anything. I had to get out of there to be myself." Yet as we talked with them, a very different picture emerged, to be later supported by sociological studies of the hippie and activist cultures. They were *not* children who grew up in families with firm rules and consistent discipline. The majority came from homes in which: 1) The parents held liberal social views which were often anti-establishment, and/or 2) the parents tended to be permissive in their child-rearing practices, and/or 3) there was a notable lack of unity between parents in decisions regarding the children, and/or 4) there was a lack of involvement and time spent in raising and guiding children.

We have listened to countless parents and children relate instances of parents giving in, against their judgment, to the wishes of their children. A teen-age girl spoke of her father: "He was always hassling me. Like I'd come in at night maybe one in the morning and he'd give me crap. I'd do the same thing the next night and I'd get the same crap again. I just got sick of it." Of course she got sick of it. Who wouldn't? Her father didn't set a limit and enforce it; he gave in and blew up. Long hair on boys provides an example of parental surrender in many homes. Whether or not long hair is good, bad, or neither here nor there isn't the issue. Many fathers and/or mothers are opposed to long hair, yet they go along with their fourteen- or fifteen-year-olds wearing locks shoulder length. Sure, they make snide remarks ("You look like a girl." "These dirty-looking long hairs," etc.) they may argue over it, or plead, or threaten, but they don't *order* a haircut and enforce the order. Many parents are troubled by doubts and fears when it comes to exercising their authority. "I don't like his long hair and dirty clothes," one worried father told us, "but I question whether I have the right to demand that he shape up; I mean, doesn't he have a right to dress as he pleases?" To which we answered: "What responsibility does he owe the other members of the family?" The notion that one's physical appearance has no effect on other family members and therefore one has no responsibility to dress in a manner which shows some concern for them is ridiculous. A father who refuses to put on a shirt and clean up before meeting his daughter's boy friend is inconsiderate and unloving. No one has a *right* to embarrass the members of his family. Parents have both the responsibility and authority to set the standards of dress and behavior. Hopefully, they have the guts to enforce them.

Until parents and other adults who hold responsibility recognize that an *authority* goes with that responsibility, and they are willing to assert that authority, not apologetically, not ambiguously, and certainly not tyrannically or irrationally, children can be expected to cry—no, to scream —for help. And they are apt to do so through rebellion.

The rebellion isn't confined to the teen-agers and college students. Twenty-year-olds may get the publicity when they fire-bomb the university computer center, but ten-year-old brothers and sisters can present problems every bit as serious. What the parents do to effect positive changes and establish a program of authority and discipline when the children are ten and five and three and fifteen will pay off when they walk the college campus at twenty. By the time children reach college age, you can't ground them, and by high school age, spanking isn't appropriate.

Today, there is rebellion among children. And it is growing. The consequences may not be as serious, but the defiant, back-talking twelve-year-old is essentially no different from the storming twenty-year-old, only younger. To pretend that it is only a "phase" the child is going through, something he will outgrow, is living on a credit card. Someday the parents as well as the child will be forced to pay for it. During the question period following a lecture we gave not long ago, someone asked if the concept of discipline wasn't outmoded. For some, yes. And with what results? For one thing, direction has shifted. Children are taking over the direction of their own lives and providing direction for other children.

The Peer Group. Peer group influence on the child has always been recognized. We can all remember how important it was to be accepted by the other kids. Whatever the gang said, we said. The gang established the code of dress, music, and behavior. And we wanted so very much to be "in." So peer group pressure is nothing new. But it *is*.

Today, the pressures are not only stronger, they take very different directions. And they represent not only an age group but a value *system*.

It may make sense to tell our child he doesn't have to do such-and-such merely because his friends are doing it, but it might be unrealistic to expect him to follow such wisdom. His peers tell him adults—perhaps especially Mother and Father—are his enemy. And as we all know, consorting with the enemy is treason and/or cowardice. It would be a mistake to underestimate the strength of such feeling among many children, especially adolescents. The pressure simply cannot be compared in strength with what existed two or more decades ago.

During our adolescence, the peer pressure was directed

toward clothes, music, our "in" language, our dancing, etc. It could also include much more and lead to trouble if we got in with the "wrong" gang. It isn't just the wrong gang today. The pressure may be toward shoplifting ("ripping off"), drugs, violence, sexual acting out, and behaviors now more or less condoned by what may be a majority of teen-agers. We do not like to accept this as so, but we should face facts: Despite what some teachers and many head-in-the-sand parents might wish to believe, these are part of the present youth scene. They are not limited to the "rough" crowd. Recently, a young nun mentioned to us a book she had planned reading. "I went to a bookstore to rip off a copy, but they were out of it!" The greater pressure today comes from a "code of the underworld" mentality. Since the young teach each other to see adults as the enemy, they develop a conspiratorial attitude which is reinforced by what they read and watch on television of older adolescents in activist uprisings. The activities have an understandable romantic appeal and an excitement. But it is not all fun and games or children playing cops and robbers ("Off the pigs!"). There is a deadly seriousness about it, and one rule accepted with the greatest seriousness is: "Don't cop out. Don't go along with the establishment." Being a "fink" by reporting rule breaking to parents and authorities is the ultimate betrayal of the youth culture. (If a drug user is reported, the one turning him in is a "narc" and considered a traitor even by most of the "straight" kids.) This sometimes frightening polarization is reinforced by some teachers who subscribe to the code and, in doing so, teach even further adult-child alienation. One teacher told his class, "Any kid who would turn in another kid isn't to be trusted." A junior high school counselor told her students, "If you think you can communicate with your parents, you have problems."

The peer group mores today take on a symbolic quality. Dress, hair, music, and language communicate a set of values which act to fractionate—by choice—the group members from the larger, square society. The child who rejects the symbolic dress, hair length, beads, language, etc. may find himself rejected by the group. This is a piece of information which can be used to advantage by the concerned parent.

If parents decide their child's peer group is, for one reason or another, an undesirable influence (not ignoring the fact that the child selected these friends and was not dragged into their circle), they may act to break it up by forcing their child to step outside the group's mores. If the group clothing, the "uniform," is blue jeans, love beads, and long hair, their teen-age son will lose his membership if he no longer wears the uniform. He will be "punished" by the group for his nonconformity, even if the nonconformity is by parental edict and not of his choosing. The hippies say they believe in total freedom for the individual, but how would they react to a crew cut in a Brooks Brothers suit? A youth drug center in southern California, which employs young "graduate" ex-drug users, has a rule which all who seek help are obliged to follow. The boys are given conventional short haircuts. All psychedelic clothing and paraphernalia are banned. They candidly admit their purpose: To give the youthful drug users a "square" image which will serve to alienate them from the hip drug crowd.

If parents are disturbed by the child's friends, they might find they can successfully employ the same technique: Change the child's wardrobe to that of the squares. This alone, of course, is not going to do it. There will also have to be increased supervision and other steps toward rational child rearing. It frequently does, however, bring some desired changes. This pressure for conformity in dress can be measured by the resistance children will raise against change. In several cases, friends have agreed to bring hip clothes to school for their friend to be changed into before first bell. Once the new image is enforced, however, it usually doesn't take long before the group begins to withdraw from the square. He no longer fits in with the old gang, and he will now have to seek admittance to a new group.

Parents and teachers are often unaware of the behavioral implications of dress and hair styles, etc. "What difference does long hair make; after all, we had our fads when we were their age." And we did. The difference is in the symbolic value. Appearance can be important in identifying the subgroup to which the child belongs or with which he hopes to identify. If the straight kids as well as the "hoods" are wearing their hair shoulder length and dressing in psychedelic clothing and love beads, it may signify nothing. Parents would be wise, however, to spend some time around the school observing appearances, and perhaps picking up some leads from teachers and counselors who, if they are perceptive as well as candid, should be able to supply information on friends, groups, cliques, and influences, both bad and good.

Several other moves may be made to break a child away from an undesirable group. They all take involvement on the part of the parents. Just giving an order to stay away is seldom enough.

If you have no clear proof the members of the clique are involved in undesirable activities, and all you have to go on is an intuitive "smell" which says something isn't quite right, you might not want to come on too strong. Curtailing visits to friends' homes and elsewhere and encouraging him (or her) to bring the friends home (where more data can be picked up) may be a first step. No point has to be made of this. Tell the child you don't like the friends he has selected (when you have nothing to back it up), and you can expect a reaction of outrage. And justifiably. No explanation should be necessary. He is simply being asked to bring his friends home instead of going elsewhere. If the children believe their friends are genuinely welcome and if they enjoy the environment their parents have created, they will want to invite them. If their friends seem reluctant to be around when adults are present, look out! It may be a further warning signal.

If you have clear evidence the gang is undesirable, you may not be able to avoid a confrontation: You lay your evidence on the table and explain why you will permit no further contact with these friends. Don't expect it to end there, however. Carrying through enforcement of this order may take just about all both parents have to give. If the child is in school with them, you cannot stop him from seeing them during school hours. You may, however, curtail the contact by making sure he leaves for school in the morning just in time to make his first class and comes home as soon as school is out, and by cutting off *all* contact, including phone, while he is at home. When you first put the order in effect, expect an eruption. And be prepared for attempts at evasions ranging from phone calls while Mother is in the other room to sneaking out after the parents are asleep. Strict supervision and surveillance are the only answer. Not the easiest or the most desirable, but what choice have you?

If the problems involving the peer group are severe, it may even be advisable to ask that the child be transferred to another school if there is one in the area. (You will then, of course, have to be on your guard to see that he doesn't fall in with a similar gang in the new school.) This may involve driving him back and forth each day as well as other adjustments in the family life, but the situation may demand it if still more serious problems are to be avoided.

We feel the following points should be restated with emphasis:

1. The peer group influence, always strong during adolescence (eleven–twenty-one), is today often a subculture marked by anti-parent, anti-establishment values, in reaction to, and reinforced by, a lack of values in the adult community.

2. The most important step in countering negative peer group values in your children is to form and present rational values and goals you hold and live by.

3. Become aware of symbolic value of the peer group

mores, dress, etc. and how you may be able to put the information to use.

4. Create an environment in the home which will make it a place your children will want to bring their friends to. Home should never be a prison.

5. Know their friends and know what your children are doing. Most children are deeply in trouble long before the parents are aware of it.

9

THE SCENE TODAY:
DRUGS

Nothing in the youth scene has touched off such hysteria, concern, misunderstanding, and misdirected activity as the reports on drug abuse among children.

The problem is real. It is growing at a frightening rate and is more widespread and serious than the majority of parents seem to recognize. It is also more pervasive than many educators and others familiar with the problem care to admit. We spoke with the vice-principal of a large middle-class suburban junior high school. "Maybe twenty or thirty of our kids," he told us, "have experimented with marijuana or some pills, but no more than that." Later, we mentioned his estimate to a narcotics officer of the police department assigned to the area. He laughed. "Who is he trying to kid? I could pick up more than twenty or thirty *pushers* at that school any lunch hour, but the juvenile hall is so overcrowded we wouldn't have any place to put them. Why does he try to snow the public?"

Why indeed? Could it be that the vice-principal and other teachers and administrators are ignorant of a problem the police describe as a "school full of 'heads'?" In one respect, this may be. To a degree, we all see what we want to see, and no school administrator wants to see a drug problem among his students any more than parents do. A drug-ridden school is a tragic, often overwhelming problem. It can spread like a brush fire and force the administrator into the role of full-time fireman. It is a job he did not seek and is poorly prepared to handle. Searching the student lockers, patrolling the rest rooms, and watching for signs and symptoms are a job for a security force, not an educator. The administrator is also keenly aware of public relations—spelled *reactions of parents.* If parents get wind the school is facing a drug problem, he knows what to expect. A very vocal group of parents, ignoring the order of their own houses, will pin the blame on the school system, the teachers, and the administrators. And who wants to take that kind of flack?

This head-in-the-sand attitude is even more evident among parents. Drug abuse is something which touches other families—most on the other side of the tracks. Not theirs. They have read of the problem, maybe even watched a TV special or two on the "stoned generation," but their sixteen-year-old son popping pills, their fourteen-year-old daughter smoking grass? Never! "I just know he never would; we've talked about it and he is dead set against dope of any kind." "Mary told me about a movie they showed at school. She was shocked that kids would fool around with drugs. I know my daughter well. She isn't the sort of girl who would be talked into trying drugs. She's levelheaded and well adjusted; she'd have no reason to."

Whether we are raising our children in rural Iowa or midtown Manhattan, the ghetto or suburbia, whether we are speaking of a sixth-grade girl or a seventeen-year-old boy, whether we have our children in a large city public high school or a small convent school for young ladies, no parent can afford such naïveté. Not today.

Old myths, images, and stereotypes are a long time dying. Marijuana, narcotics, and dangerous drugs were used by juveniles twenty and thirty years ago. Then, however, it was far away from the white middle-class world. It was a problem of the ethnic minorities in the ghettos. The middle class knew it existed. But then, so did malaria in the tropics and concubinage in China. It wasn't their problem. Well, it is today. Drugs have spread from the ghettos to the "better class" neighborhoods, the college campuses, suburban high schools and junior highs. And pills are now being passed on the playground of your neighborhood grammar school.

Statistics on the incidence of drug use don't help much in understanding its scope. Any percentages we might quote today can be counted on to be invalid by the time this book reaches the reader. Not only are the numbers increasing, the problem is spreading to communities where it was unknown a very short time ago. Church youth groups as well as hippie communes have their pot parties. The high school football star, the student body president, the homecoming queen, and the honor student are almost as apt to be "popping reds," "shooting speed," or "smoking grass" as the long-haired rock musician.

If we hope to cope with the situation of drugs among our children, we must discard the common beliefs:

1. *The schoolteachers know about these things and they'd let the parents know if they suspected anything.* This is unrealistic. Why should we expect a teacher to know each of thirty or more children better than we know one child? The high school history teacher has groups of students filing in and out of the classroom several times each day. Willie, sitting there in the back of the classroom, looks sleepy, his eyes half-closed. Is he coming down with a cold? Did he stay up late last night watching television? Or is he high on barbiturates? Marylou's counselor might suspect the girl of being turned on by "meth-tabs"; she might even question her about it. But once Marylou denies it, where can the counselor go from there? To take her suspicions to the parents might be to invite trouble. She has no proof. The parents might blow up at their daughter being "unjustly" accused. One high school principal stated his policy this way: "We can't search them when they come to school, and we cannot run blood tests on them. When it's an obvious O.D. (overdose of drugs) we call an ambulance or send them home. What more can we do?"

2. *I've read up on what to look for, those signs of drug use, and I'd know if he were taking anything.* It is true

that under the influence of *some* drugs, taken in sufficient quantity, *some,* but not all users, will show those signs we all hear about—change in pupillary size and response to light, drowsiness, runny nose and eyes, loss of appetite, etc., but frequently the symptoms will appear only with heavy dosage. And would any parent want to wait until then? By the time the symptoms appear (if, in fact, they ever do), the child may be a full-fledged member of the drug culture. This isn't to suggest you should not stay aware of your children's condition—including any possible symptoms they may show—just don't rely on an apparent absence of symptoms as proof your child is not "turning on."

3. *We live in a small community. We know all his friends and we are sure there are no "pushers" around here.* If the drug pusher ever resembled the heavy in those old movies—snapbrim hat over eyes, dark shirt, turned-up coat collar—lurking on the corner near the high school, he doesn't any more. Now, the pusher—if that name even applies—is apt to be the friendly sandy-haired kid who comes over to study for the biology test with your son, or the cute little girl who double-dated with your daughter to her first high school formal. It may even be, as in one recent case we came across, an eleven-year-old junior swimming champion (arrested with a sizable quantity of drugs she planned to sell to her friends). The merchants at the top of this illegal drug trade are not, of course, school children, but the ones giving and selling drugs to children from grammar school through college are their friends and classmates. They are not, for the most part, adventures in free enterprise; profit is seldom their motive. They buy a quantity of grass or pills, sell most of it to their friends, and have enough left over for themselves—their profit. Of one thing you can be very sure: The teenage boy or girl interested in obtaining drugs or grass knows where to go to get them—any time during the school year and all summer vacation—to his classmates!

4. *Only the mixed-up, emotionally disturbed, or un-*

happy youngsters are turning to drugs. Twenty or thirty
years ago this might have been true. Not today. Drug use
is as much a part of our children's generation as liquor is
of ours. Certainly, the unhappy or disturbed child is more
likely to turn to drugs and to develop a drug dependency
as a means of coping with his problems just as some adults
come to rely on alcohol, tranquilizers, or sleeping pills.
Drug use, however, is not at all confined to troubled children. The drugs are readily available to all. There is
widespread acceptance of most drugs with little or no
social censure for their use (even the "acid heads" and
"speed freaks" are seldom rejected for their habits and
almost never reported by their fellow students).

5. *But if kids can be made aware of the danger of these
drugs, won't they stay away from them?* At some point
in time not too long ago, this might have been the answer.
About thirty years ago, audiences sat spellbound through
scare-horror movies like *Marijuana Madness.* Today, it
would be merely "camp." Some adults still have faith in
drug education programs. But how many children are buying what the adults have been trying to sell re drugs? In
the first place, they are not as naïve as adults might believe (or want to believe). A policeman was lecturing a
high school class on drugs and their abuse. To help them
identify marijuana if they should come across it, he passed
around a plate on which he had placed two "joints." When
the plate came back to him, *three* joints rested on it.

The first concern of the middle class was with marijuana.
Long used in the ghettos and among jazz musicians, the
use spread during the early 1950s to the beat generation
of San Francisco's North Beach and New York's East Vil-
lage. From there, grass moved to the college campus, first
among the graduate students, later to the undergraduates.
By the time it took roots in the high schools, parents pan-
icked. Most parents knew little or nothing of marijuana.
They may still have remembered those movie melodramas.
Educators were no better informed. Neither were the police. Even physicians were pitifully lacking in their knowl-

edge of the drug. The fact was—and *is*—not much of anything was known of the effects of *Cannibis sativa*, marijuana. Even today, we have more evidence of danger in cigarette smoking than we do of any risks in smoking "grass."

Adults reacted out of ignorance. They still do. They told their children, "It leads to heroin addiction." "People have committed murder and rape when high on marijuana." "It causes psychosis." Harry Anslinger, the prohibition agent turned federal narcotics chief, now retired, had done his work well. His scare tactics had supplied parents with a large body of misinformation. And it backfired. When it came to marijuana, the children turned out to know more than their parents. They knew grass (that their parents called "reefers" or "tea") didn't turn one into a junkie, rapist, or murderer, that it didn't make you lose your mind, your virtue, or your virility. The parents and teachers had lied! And if they lied about marijuana, isn't it possible they lied about all those other drugs they warned against? Why believe them at all? What do they know? (Answer: Maybe not much!) When LSD and the other psychedelic drugs broke on the scene in the early 1960s, the parents were even less prepared. Here were powerful mind-altering drugs, and they knew absolutely nothing about them. The drug education teachers were no better informed. They warned the students of the dangerous new drugs and gave emphasis to their warnings through horror story rumors of bad trips ending in suicide or murder. But by that time, the kids were already dropping "acid" or knew classmates who were and they knew better (or thought they did). When we now try to warn them of the serious dangers of "speed," "reds," "blues," "yellows," "rainbows," "uppers," "downers" and narcotics, they throw the switch turning us off. What do adults know anyway.

If we are to have any influence on our children when it comes to drugs, we must know what we are talking about and be honest in presenting what we know. Children want guidance today as much as they ever did, maybe more. But they are less easily fooled, thanks to impact of the mass media. When we were their age, parents might have been able to convince children masturbation causes insanity or poor eyesight. Not today. They know better. They likewise know a lot about drugs, often more than parents realize, and frequently more than the parents. As in the classic story of the father who called his son in for a serious father-son talk. "Son, it's time we have a little talk about sex." To which the boy replied, "Sure, Dad, what would you like to know?" Today's teenager is not going to be patronized by parents and teachers, which is what they were saying when they returned the third joint to the police officer.

What they often lack are hard facts on the long-range effects of the various drugs and some valid, rational reasons for staying off them. They know, for example, that most kids are not likely to get hooked on the more popular drugs if they are used in moderation. They know that most of these drugs—amphetamines, barbiturates, and marijuana—can be taken in moderate amounts without fear of detectable symptoms. And they know something else: That it is the adults, far more than their generation, who make up the "drug culture." Their parents even use the same drugs they warn against. One difference: The adults are able to obtain the pills by prescription. They warn children against amphetamines—"bennies," "dex," "speed," "uppers"—but Mother has a refillable prescription for a similar drug in her bathroom medicine cabinet. She calls them her "diet pills." What the kids call "reds," the parents use each night: the sleeping pills. If the adolescent gets upset or nervous he is told to "calm down" or "snap out of it." Mother complains the kids are driving her up the wall and she pops a tranquilizer in her mouth. When Dad comes home uptight, he mixes a double martini. If we hope to convince our children drugs are a poor way of attempting to cope with life's problems, we should make sure we are not showing them a picture of our own membership in the adult drug culture.

6. *He (or she) is around the house most of the time when he isn't in school. I don't see when he would have the chance to take drugs.* How long does it take to swallow a pill? Or smoke one joint? Those pictures of the pot party with kids lying around the floor of a dimly lit room "stoned" are not "where it's at." Given the time and place, they might have the party. But they don't need it. Much of the "pill popping" today takes place virtually under the noses of the teachers and parents. A fifteen-year-old girl told us of how she baked marijuana into cookies in her home economics class. "It was a blast, man. The whole class turned on and that square teacher didn't even pick up on what was happening." Many students drop pills before first period and again during lunch hour. Grass may be smoked going or coming from school or, if more adventuresome, in the lavatories between classes. Parents frequently permit children to entertain friends in their rooms, thus another opportunity. Group outings, especially those with limited adult supervision, are close to an open door to drug use. A minister told us it was necessary for him to close the weekend teen-age bible camp. "We knew the kids were smoking pot. We felt there wasn't much harm in it and we couldn't do much to stop it, but when they started on pills, we knew we couldn't assume the responsibility and risk having some kid freak out."

No parent can watch a child twenty-four hours a day. Nor can a parent rest secure in the feeling "I know my child; he's not the type to try drugs." This isn't 1940. And there is no "type." Whether you live in San Francisco or Sioux City, drugs are a big part of the youth scene. Parents can realistically make only one assumption: *Given the opportunity and encouragement of the peer group, the child will experiment with drugs.*

While nothing will provide ironclad insurance against drug involvement, there are steps parents can take to reduce at least the risk of serious drug involvement:

1. *Know your child.* The most obvious, but easier said than done. Communication plays a big part in it. Communication between the parents, comparing their observations on the child, his activities, and friends, is every bit as important as communication between parent and child. Two heads and two observers are better than one. If you come to know well his moods, his reactions, and his behavior patterns, you will have a good chance of picking up changes which might signal drug use. It isn't infallible. But we frequently find where children have been deeply involved in drugs, the symptoms were evident long before the child was finally caught. The parents were either totally unaware of the signs or had dismissed them as "a phase he's going through," "a part of being a teen-ager," or a minor physical problem, a cold or "feeling out of sorts." You cannot know your child *too* well. He is an individual. To know a child, we must continually work to know his views, his frustrations, his dreams, his friends, his interests, and activities. There will always be a secret world which is his alone, and that is how it should be. You can learn a great deal of his world, however, by building and maintaining good communication. And by continual observation. The key to keeping the door open is the ability to express genuine interest in his world and in him. If it isn't genuine, the child will know it and recognize it for what it is: prying into his activities in order to keep him in line. When that happens, the door will slam shut.

2. *Know drugs and what they do.* If we don't know more about drugs than our children do (and more than the typical teacher of a class in drug education), we can expect to be ignored when we bring up the subject. They want to know about drugs, but they want straight facts, not rumors. And not sermons. For several years, adults have been warning them of the dangers of cigarette smoking. They have been told the facts and many of them have become vocal opponents of cigarettes (as some smoking parents can attest). If we start leveling with them about drugs, we may find them turning away from them.

Do we have, for example, a rational argument to present against the use of marijuana, one we can back with proven evidence? Try telling a teen-ager it can cause insanity or impotency (as one elderly doctor tried to suggest), and the battle will be lost before it begins. What if our children tell us alcohol is a drug with more proven harmful effects than grass? They're right. And if we try to convince them marijuana is worse, we will be talking nonsense, at least from what research findings we presently have.

This doesn't mean, however, that we are left with no argument and that we must give marijuana use our blessing. There is no clear-cut evidence (at present) that marijuana is a serious danger to either physical or mental health when used in moderate amounts. It is perhaps not as deleterious to one's health as alcohol and nowhere near the danger we find in the pills (amphetamines or barbiturates) or narcotics. Long overdue research is being conducted and authorities are taking a second look at a problem which may have been created by hysterical laws which lumped marijuana in with heroin and cocaine.

We can tell our children: (a) Since marijuana is still illegal, they run the risk of arrest if it is found in their possession. What this might mean in terms of possible confinement varies (and with no rhyme or reason) from one jurisdiction to another, and one judge to another. But even with probation or suspended sentence, the young offender will have a mark on his record which could seriously hinder his future life plans. (b) Purchase of marijuana places him within a broader drug environment, and exposes him to those dealing in and using more dangerous drugs. While there is no evidence that it *leads* to heroin or other hard drug use, due to the hard line laws which place it within the drug culture, marijuana can open the door to something much worse. (c) Driving an automobile and some other activities while under the influence of marijuana are definitely dangerous. Like alcohol, marijuana is an intoxicant. Time and depth perception are affected. Visual per-

ception may be altered. The child should be made aware
that even if he is not driving the car, if he and his friends
turn on to grass, the kid behind the wheel may be in no
shape to drive.

The other "highs" ranging from glue sniffing to heroin
are something else again. They have been proven dangerous, and there is plenty of hard, cold facts to back up
any arguments against their use. Just make sure you have
the facts. A talk with the family doctor may give you the
information you need. And no family should wait until they
suspect something is going on to seek information. Your
doctor isn't going to be shocked by the question. Also,
there are several good books and pamphlets available. *The
Pleasure Seekers: The Drug Crisis, Youth and Society* by
Joel Fort, M.D. (Grove Press, New York; 1970), a na-
tionally recognized authority on drug abuse, is one of the
best.

3. *Exercise surveillance and control.* This is the hard-
est step of all. And it is where so many parents fall down.
No parent wants to take on the role of superspy or parole
officer. "You act like you don't trust me" is enough to make
most parents back off, or at least try to defend against the
charge.

But should we be defensive? Does it show a mistrust
of the twenty-year-old private that we don't permit him to
lead the regiment into battle? Do we show a lack of trust
in the four-year-old when we won't let him excavate his
sand pile with dynamite caps? If we trusted completely
the judgments of children and discounted the wisdom and
prudence which come from age and experience, we might
permit thirteen-year-olds to drive, fourteen-year-olds to
marry, and fifteen-year-olds to sign contracts.

We don't expect children to recognize fully the possible
consequences of their actions. We don't trust the child to
make rational decisions at all times. (We don't expect it
even of an adult.) We also don't expect him to be completely open in revealing his plans and activities, especially when it might work to his disadvantage by causing

his parents to step in and set limits. We didn't tell our parents everything. Did you? Why should we expect our children to be different? The parent who says, "My child would never lie to me," has no understanding of the child —of any child. When it is to his advantage—either in seeking pleasure or avoiding pain—he may lie. In this respect, he is no different from the adult. What do we tell the traffic cop when he asks, "How fast were you going?"

How much should a parent spy on a child (if we must call it "spying")? One suitable answer might be "As much as necessary for the child's welfare." We might also answer, "It depends on what, if anything, you suspect." But a distinction should be drawn between surveillance and spying. The snooping parent, who listens in on phone calls, opens the child's mail, or reads the diary, will soon discover *nothing*. Whatever, if anything, the child may be up to, he will learn to keep quiet about it on the phone and not leave any incriminating notes around. Furthermore, such parental tactics are a sure way of widening the parent-child gap.

Surveillance will only serve to keep you in touch with what may be going on if your child is unaware of it. The spy who makes himself obvious is a failure. If you are going to check over his room, don't make an announcement of "regular room inspections." Don't let it be known you intend doing so at all. If he is warned ahead of time, any drugs he might have had will be moved to the school locker or elsewhere. Once you let it be known you have checked, your advantage is lost. If you turn up something in the search of which you don't approve, it makes sense to confront him with the evidence *only* if you feel serious steps are called for. Mother may be upset on finding girlie magazines under her teen-age son's mattress (although she shouldn't be), but girlie magazines are not hard drugs. The wisest move under the circumstances would be to not force a confrontation. Carefully replace the magazines and go on with the periodic checks.

And if drugs are uncovered? First of all, accept the fact

that the drug is illegal. This may seem obvious, yet we have many times spoken with parents who were more than willing to accept the most farfetched explanations for the presence of what were undoubtedly illegal drugs. A father found a bag of greenish shredded leaves together with a package of cigarette papers behind a box on a high closet shelf in his son's room. He asked the boy about it. "He told me it was a turkish tobacco he got from a friend. He was trying out smoking, just as we all did at that age. I gave it back to him but I told him I thought he was too young to smoke." A mother and father faced their fifteen-year-old daughter with some capsules they found in her jacket pocket. She told them they were cold capsules given her by a friend. It makes sense to assume that if it *looks* like a drug, it *is* a drug, and probably an illegal one. If he or she sticks to the "cold capsule" story, have the drug identified. Your family doctor can tell you what it is. Every drug on the market has a distinctive appearance and can be identified by looking through a copy of the *Physicians' Desk Reference* (*PDR*).

The most important point for parents: We cannot afford to underestimate drug usage. What a few years ago was a minor problem on college campuses is now in the grade schools. Recently, we were asked by a mother if we would see her son in psychotherapy. The boy, a nine-year-old, was "mainlining" speed! None of us can make the mistake of seeing it as "somebody else's child, not mine." If your teen-age son or daughter is "average," he or she has already experimented with drugs, or will soon. Even with a considerable degree of awareness and control, we may not prevent it. If we attempt to ignore it, we encourage it.

10

THE SCENE TODAY:
SEX AND THE NEW MORALITY

Shortly after World War II a new chapter opened on sexual attitudes and behavior in the Western world. We have moved faster and further in changing our sexual mores in the past quarter century than at any period in history. Whether we are headed toward a healthier sexual liberation or toward moral decay is a question which can be answered only by personal values. The hysterics who draw parallels with the decline in the Roman Empire or who paint glowing pictures of a world free of wars and sexual hang-ups through the new liberation produce considerable heat but little light. Of one thing we can be certain: The attitudes and assumptions of yesterday simply do not apply today.

Something else should be equally apparent: The majority of parents are unaware of just how the sexual revolution has affected their children. They are trying to understand today's sex scene within yesterday's frame of reference.

We recently took part in a day long "rap session" with high school students. Present was a young social worker who seemed to be trying very hard to gain acceptance by the students. He argued with some force for the sexual "rights" of their generation. "I feel you kids have the right to the pill with or without your parents' consent, married or not," he told them. One of the younger girls answered him with a sneer. "What makes you think we can't get anything we want?" And for at least the more sophisticated ones, she was speaking a truth. The social worker, although a young man, stood on the other side of a generation gap.

How much change has taken place during the past twenty, ten, and even five years cannot be measured with any accuracy. Now and then a magazine article appears in which the author claims the changes are exaggerated. The piece carries the message "Don't worry; kids are not doing anything more than we did at their age." These words may soothe some apprehensive parents, but they do not represent the realities of today's youth culture. Things are *not* the same. And the changes promise to be still greater in the coming decade. Statistical evidence in this area is bound to be suspect. Any study of human activity in an area as emotionally loaded as sex carries a risk of sampling error and the implicit question "How do you know the parties questioned were telling the truth?" One recent study should win a prize for bias and/or gullibility and/or stupidity. Several officers of the Los Angeles Police Department set out to determine the acceptable community standards regarding nudity and sexual acts on stage and in movies. Standing outside supermarkets, and after first identifying themselves as police officers, they asked customers whether they approved or disapproved of each of a list of sexual acts depicted! Any bias of the investigator may influence the results of a study. Attitudes and personalities are important when asking questions on sex. And the wording of the questions may significantly influence the answers. When Kinsey, Pomeroy and their associates published their initial studies on sexual behavior, they touched off considerable statistical nit-picking which tended to obscure the great contributions they made. We have no intention of falling into a trap of debating whether 79 per cent or 66 per cent of high school age children do such-and-such. We will rely on words like "most" and "the majority" to mean some percentage above 50 per cent in published studies. We are not so much concerned with what percentage, whether 90 per cent or 10 per cent, of

children of a certain age group are engaged in an identified sexual activity as we are in examining the group attitudes toward the activity, since it is the attitudes—
acceptance, encouragement, censure, etc.—which form the
overall "climate" in which our children live and grow. Just
what is today's youth scene when it comes to sex?

1. *Most boys and girls have engaged in boy-girl sexual
acts to orgasm before they have completed high school.*

2. *The majority of teen-agers do not believe sexual intercourse prior to marriage is morally wrong.*

3. *In at least some areas of the country, it is estimated
that half or more of all brides are pregnant at the time of
their wedding, and the percentages are increasing.*

4. *The majority of high school age children of both
sexes believe sex between unmarried partners is acceptable "if the boy and girl are in love."*

5. *Most high schoolers find nothing "wrong" with overnight outings (e.g., ski trips) which would include both
sexes staying in the same accommodations without supervision.*

6. *Most high school girls said they would not be
shocked or surprised to learn their best friend was having
frequent intercourse with a boy friend.*

7. *When asked to describe their ideal future college
roommate, over half the high school students of both sexes
specified someone of the opposite sex.*

In speaking with a group of thirty boys and girls, members of a Catholic youth group (a group we might expect
would hold relatively conservative sexual views), we were
struck by the candor with which they discussed both sexual behavior and attitudes and the extent to which it de-
parted from the traditional morality of parents and church.
No member of the group, for example, defended the
teaching of premarital sex as sinful. (One girl laughingly
said, "If our folks knew where we stood, they'd never let
us out of the house.") What impressed us, however, was
the *morality* which was present throughout their statements of position. They did not argue for unbridled sexual

license. A fifteen-year-old girl, who freely admitted to having sexual relations once or twice each week with her steady boy friend, felt that "a girl who has sex with every guy around must have some bad hang-ups." Whether sex is right or wrong, in the opinion of most of them, is determined by the *quality of the relationship*. If the relationship is loving, and there is no exploitation involved, sex is *good* and *right*. If it is not an expression of love, it is *wrong*. But "wrong," as they use the word, does not mean sinful or immoral. The war in Vietnam is immoral; sex between lovers is not. The act can be immoral if love is gone. As one girl put it: "I think sex between most parents is immoral. My mom and dad have one of their fights, then go to bed. That's filthy!"

This moral code based upon existence of a loving and meaningful relationship may be transitional. Predictions are difficult in a time of rapid change. Increasingly, we hear expressions from adolescents of an even more open, free, and what might be called "casual" approach to sex. It has been called "sexual anarchy" by more than one critic, but that is another pejorative term which is far from illuminating. This more liberal view is essentially amoral. Sex, any sex, engaged in by mutual consent cannot be said to be immoral. The advocates oppose any legal or moral restraints on sexual expression, excepting rape and child molesting. While not encouraging any one form of sexual expression, they defend the individual's right to seek whatever is desirable—homosexual, heterosexual, within or without marriage. "We should get rid of labels which condemn people, words like 'perverted' and 'immoral' just because some people may have sex interests which differ from ours," a college coed told us. "Why should anyone try to say what is right and wrong in sex; it should be up to the individual." As she, and others who hold similar views, see it, sex may be better if the couple have a "meaningful relationship" but sex is sex, an enjoyable physical act under any of a variety of circumstances and with any of a number of possible partners. They may be speaking for the generation entering adolescence five years from now. No one can know.

Regardless of what individual children may be doing, there can be no doubt there has been a major change in attitudes. Twenty years ago, the high school girl who found herself in "trouble" was shuffled off by her parents to stay with a distant relative or take residence in a home for unwed mothers. Despite efforts to hush up the disgrace, the news invariably leaked out and the parents and the girl became the talk of the community. If rumors spread that a girl had had relations with her boy friend, she might pick up the label "tramp" and get known as an "easy make." Every high school boy knew who "those girls" were on the campus. The nice girls were repeatedly cautioned to "be careful of your reputation." Most parents still hold such views. But not the children. Their attitude is likely to be: "It is nobody else's business what somebody does; if someone wants to have sex, it should be up to them."

There may still be pockets of sexual conservatism among youth in some areas of the country, notably the southern states and rural Midwest, but nearly everywhere the changes have been dramatic. If parents hope to influence the sexual activities and attitudes of their children, they must be willing to accept the fact that attitudes have changed. They don't necessarily have to condone the newer views. And they certainly should not resign parenthood in the face of them. But they do have to face the fact that in this changed world, the old arguments, prohibitions, and group mores cannot be relied upon to reinforce their sexual morality.

Not too many years ago, parents had some success teaching their daughters most of the following:

1. Virginity is the greatest gift a bride can give her husband.

2. A boy is interested in only one thing, and it is a girl's responsibility to keep a boy in line.

3. A boy loses respect for a girl who permits him sexual liberties.

4. A girl who becomes pregnant before marriage will live in shame and regret the rest of her life—even if she marries the baby's father.

5. If a girl permits a boy sexual liberties, she can expect him to spread it all over town by his bragging.

6. If a couple have sex, no matter what they may do to prevent it, there is always considerable risk of pregnancy.

7. A girl who would discuss sexual matters in the presence of a boy is probably not a "nice" girl.

8. Every boy will make passes, but a boy most admires the girl who says "No."

9. Any sex before marriage is seriously sinful.

Boys were taught the same things, but there was often some concession, even if unverbalized, to the "double standard."

Today, not one of these arguments stands much chance of being accepted by teen-agers. Most of these arguments were built on what was taken to be the attitudes of middle-class society: How do boys see girls who "do" vs. girls who "don't?" How does the girl see herself? How will her friends see the girl who "gives in?"

The answers to these questions we were given when we were going through the adolescent years may have been valid then, but not now. The knowledgeable teen-ager of today knows better. Virginity, as one girl put it, is a "commodity with no sales value." They know their friends are having sex with their "steadies" and they think no less of them. A girl friend gets pregnant and they are likely to plan a baby shower for her.

As for the fear of pregnancy? The rate of unwed teen-age pregnancies has been climbing steadily despite the fact that the girl of fifteen today knows more about contraception than her parents did five years after they married. Apparently, any fear they may have is not strong, or maybe more than a few teen-age girls are seeking to become mothers at such an early age. We have talked with a number of girls who admitted to trying to get pregnant "so I can have someone to love" . . . "because I want my boy friend's baby" . . . "so I can get away from home" . . . etc.

The danger of venereal disease doesn't seem to stop many of them. The risk is greater today among that age group than ever before. It has reached epidemic proportions and has become a major public health problem, but how does anyone convince a sixteen-year-old boy that the sweet little girl who sings in the high school choir may have gonorrhea? Or persuade a very much in love girl her boy friend may be infected? The present danger of venereal disease may—just *may*—persuade the young to take precautions against VD, and education may encourage them to seek early treatment if they become infected. Hopefully, something will prove effective in curbing the spread. It is highly unlikely, however, that scare tactics will deter sexual activity among today's children. Whether of sin, pregnancy, disgrace, or disease, today's children are unafraid.

An Approach to Sex. Every parent has some idea of what he wants to give to his child in the way of sexual information and, more important, sexual attitudes. Conveying it is something else. If many adults were really honest with themselves and others—including their children—they would admit that their primary goal in giving sexual direction to the young is to keep the kids from doing *anything* sexually until they are safely within the bonds of matrimony. Sex-education-in-the-school advocates frequently speak of "life education" but go on to cite alarming figures of teen-age pregnancy as if a knowledge of how conception occurs will *deter* any such activities. (This is not, however, an indictment of sex education or sex educators as a whole. Organizations such as SIECUS* have been doing an excellent job of calling the public's atten-

* Sex Information and Education Council of the United States.

tion to the need for sound, rational programs throughout the school years.) Those opposed to sex education fear that a knowledge of how conception occurs will *lead* to such activities. How to keep the kids from "doing it" has been something of an obsessive question plaguing parents for centuries. Traditionally they have tried to scare them out of it—one way or another. Or make sex so disgusting and "dirty" the child, and later the *adult*, will be repulsed by it. The damage done by such anti-sexualism is incalculable. Ask any counselor or psychotherapist.

Teaching healthy sexual attitudes is the parents' job. The schools can't do it, nor can the Scouts, YMCA, or the churches. It can't be done with books, audio-visual aids, or a chat with the family doctor. The buck stops with the parents. Whether they think it through or not, whether or not they are even aware of doing so, the parents are going to teach sexual attitudes. The attitudes may be wholesome, or they may be sick. It will depend entirely on the attitudes held by the parents. Children are seldom deceived by words which fail to reveal what the parent feels on a "gut level." Dr. William Masters, the noted sex researcher, said it very well: "The best sex education a child can receive is when he watches Daddy pat Mommie on the fanny and sees that Mommie enjoys it." Hence, the first step toward the sex education of your child:

1. *Make a thorough examination of your own sexual attitudes and the quality of the sexual relationship between you and your spouse.* The few hours the two of you spend in such an "in-depth" discussion may prove to be one of the most important you may ever have in determining the direction of your child-rearing activity. And it may also be the most important step toward the marriage you both desire. If sex leaves anything to be desired—for either or both of you—stop right there and do something about it. Don't kid yourself into believing you can keep your problems behind the bedroom door. You can't. If you feel embarrassed discussing sex with your child—or your spouse—you probably should recognize such embarrass-

ment as an indication of a problem of sexual attitudes which you would not want passed on to your children. Whatever you do, don't try to sweep it under the rug. It is too important to your child's future happiness to be ignored. If you feel the problem cannot be worked through between the two of you, by all means seek help from a competent marriage counselor, psychologist, or psychiatrist.

2. *Be willing to express the meaning and rewards you have found in sex, not just the facts of sex and reproduction.* As progressive as some sex education programs in some schools may be, you are not likely to find one which can legitimately be called *sex* education. It is more apt to be a course in the anatomy and physiology of reproduction with perhaps (but not always) some information on contraception and venereal disease. It will not include much, if anything, on various sexual acts, means of arousal, erogenous areas of the body, etc., and the educator brave enough or foolhardy enough to attempt to introduce a course covering such material would undoubtedly be nailed to the schoolhouse wall. In most school districts, the teachers would find their jobs in jeopardy if they were to speak at all of the sex act as a pleasurable experience (from parents who don't find much pleasure in the act and certainly don't want their children trying out such pleasures).

Sex is not, however, a simple matter of biology—nor reproduction. Sex bears a relationship to reproduction similar to the relationship gourmet eating bears to digestion, yet the emphasis in most sex education lectures is entirely on reproduction and the anatomy of the reproductive system. This isn't enough. It isn't even the important dimension of sex education. One could have the knowledge of a professional physiologist or gynecologist and still hold unhealthy sexual attitudes. The sex educators can't be blamed, and perhaps it is just as well that they keep subjective feelings out of their courses. But the parents should not hesitate to let their children know that sex is something

pretty special, one of life's most pleasurable experiences.
That means more than merely saying that sex is "good"
or "it is a way in which Mommie and Daddy say 'I love
you.'" Parents often fear that "making it sound too good"
will spur the child to try it out. They needn't worry. Children have a sexual drive which increases with the onset
of adolescence. Sexual pleasure they will discover on their
own. They do need to know that their parents find this
pleasure *with each other* and that they accept it and are
at ease in expressing it. It goes a long way toward development of wholesome attitudes.

3. *Accept the child's sexuality.* The child begins exploring his or her body, including his sexual anatomy, before
toilet training or weaning occurs. It continues all through
childhood and can become a powerful preoccupation during adolescence. (A recent study found that the majority
of students admitted they were thinking of things sexual
when "daydreaming" during class.) If the parents treat
sexual exploration with self and/or other children as something "horrid" and a punishable offense, rather than as a
normal part of the child's education and development, the
child's future sexual attitudes may be adversely affected—
seriously so.

Parents can explain to a child that playing "doctor" or
other sexual exploration games may upset other parents
and that for this reason—but no other—should not continue. To punish him (or her) for his normal sexuality,
however, is a serious mistake. Masturbation is a normal
part of adolescence for both sexes and it should be treated
as such; ignore it. Many adults carry vivid memories of
explosive ugly scenes that followed being caught in the
act of masturbating. They were made to feel dirty and
abnormal. It was even called an "unnatural act" and a
"sin of self-abuse." The effects of this kind of "teaching"
can be devastating. Topics touching on areas of sexuality—
sexual acts, feelings, desires—should be allowed to come
up in conversation between parent and child with the same
openness and spontaneity as, say, talk of sports or school

activity. And treated with the same spirit of naturalness. This is difficult for many parents, raised as they were in an age of sexual repression, but no more important sex education can be given to the child than through this free exchange which communicates, "I recognize that you have these feelings just as we all do—and the feelings are natural and good."

4. *Sex doesn't come naturally; it must be taught.* Much as we hear talk of the sexual revolution and the sexual sophistication of youth, and the young are, without doubt, more knowledgeable in the area of sex than most of us were at their age, we still find large gaps in their knowledge whenever we speak to groups of adolescents, even those preparing for marriage. Sex education courses have helped some, but as we said, they are not courses in sex education; they are courses in the anatomy of reproduction. Too many adults seem to assume that if the child is supplied with the basic information as to where babies come from, the rest will be a matter of "doing what comes naturally." Nothing could be further from the truth. No area of human existence is more complex psychologically, more bound up in emotion, more potentially traumatic. And in the culture in which we live, nothing is more burdened down with taboos and misinformation.

How much information should the child be given and at what age? The fact that the question is asked at all probably attests to the anxiety we parents feel in the matter of sex. After all, we don't ask such questions when we are talking of teaching the child how to care for a pet, play baseball, or work multiplication tables. Why should sex be the exception? Countless authorities have advised parents to "answer the child's questions as they arise, but to give only such information as is necessary at that age." Whatever that means! The advice only adds to problems where problems should not exist. The child should be given information on sex as freely and completely as one would give information on geography or the workings of a jet airplane. Don't worry! If he can't follow all of it or becomes bored by a detailed answer, you'll know it. The five-year-old isn't likely to follow a lengthy explanation of the workings of a jet propulsion engine either. If it gets too complicated for him, he will show it in his actions and expression and his parent may feel "I've lost him." So at that point you stop. The same should hold true for sex. There should be no age at which *truth* and knowledge are withheld. Parents often fear that sex information will lead the child to try "experimenting" with what he or she has learned. The child may, but probably no more so than if he proceeds "by trial and error." In any case, should the sexual games of little children really be a serious concern?

When you give your child sexual information, be sure it is *sexual* information, not solely information on reproduction. There are a few score books on the market designed to teach children (or to help parents teach children) how babies are born, how birds and bees procreate, or "how God makes little boys and girls." Not one we have come across talks honestly of sex. You know and we know husbands and wives don't have sex only at such times as they wish to conceive a child, and only in order to conceive a child. Yet this is what the child is taught when Mother says something like "This is the way God designed things so that mommies and daddies could have babies." Even in this "enlightened" age we talk to early adolescents who believe couples "do it" only when they plan a child. What a distorted picture of sex! Why not tell the child Mommie and Daddy do it because it feels good, because it is a way of saying "I love you," and because it is a lot of fun—and Mommie and Daddy do it frequently? And by all means give enough information about the sex act (acts) that the child can understand what really happens. To understand the sex act, a girl must understand what an erection is, and both a boy and girl need to know what occurs during sexual excitation up to and including ejaculation (many children grow up with the idea that the man urinates in the woman).

In 1967, we authored a book, *The Freedom of Sexual*

Love, on the Christian concept of sexuality. Many parents asked us at what age we felt a child should be allowed to read the book. Our answer: At whatever age the child is interested in reading it. The answer would be the same for any book of a similar nature. If the book contains misinformation or what the parents judge to be distorted values they probably will throw the book out; if it has valid information, why shouldn't the child be permitted to read it if he is interested (most younger children won't be; our children don't even read their parents' books on sex and marriage). If you are not sure of your own information, you might pick up one or two authoritative books. And after you have read them, don't be afraid of leaving them around. Knowledge never harmed anyone—not even a child.

5. *Present sexual morality with reason.* Children are not —repeat, not—going to accept a sexual morality which is little more than "you can—you can't." In talking with many, many teen-agers we have found only one approach they are willing to accept—or even consider: What is the *responsible* thing to do.

A seventeen-year-old boy may understand that having sex with his fifteen-year-old girl friend who has strong sexual inhibitions and may have sex only to keep him and will suffer from subsequent guilt feelings is an irresponsible and exploitive act. He may not accept the argument that sex before marriage is wrong. The fifteen-year-old girl may accept the argument that since she is not yet willing to take the responsibilities of pregnancy and child rearing and is not under the protection of a "sure" contraceptive (the pill or intra-uterine device), sexual intercourse is an irresponsible gamble. Just don't try to convince her that the loss of her virginity will cause her untold anguish. Regardless of the sexual morality of the parents, children today are coldly pragmatic and rational and are not apt to buy any "moral" arguments which are not firmly rooted in "hard logic." They are more probably willing to accept an argument which is realistically based on the consequences of their actions—provable consequences—than any position based upon "moral" judgment. Just make sure your arguments are sound and can be backed up with factual points. If not, you may never know it, but they will be shot down by your children—who live in a different, more pragmatic, world.

In the parent's role in the area of the child's sexual development, one side of the coin is *education,* the other side is *supervision.* And here again, our society has given way to a youth culture with responsibility for whatever limits exist being assumed by the children. Children establish the mores of the peer group and the parents fall in line in giving their support. What is popular becomes what is accepted. In less than two decades, the sexual mores of adolescents have moved downward in age almost four to five years. Behavior which was typical of sixteen- and seventeen-year-olds has become established for twelve-year-olds, and often with at least a passive acceptance by the adult society. This has added a good measure to the already great pressures of early adolescence.

For some reason (perhaps the need for vicarious popularity and sexual conquest) it is mothers who are most responsible for this shift downward in sexual sophistication. They not only encourage their daughters, they virtually push them into the dating—and *seduction*—game before the girls are ready to give up dolls. Seventh graders are fitted with falsies, eye shadow, and bouffant hair styles, and sent off to catch a boy. Of course Mother doesn't admit to such a motive; she says simply, "All the girls her age are doing it." And for the majority, she may be correct. The latest fad in our area among the seventh grade *femme fatales* is pierced ears to go along with the almost black eyeshadow. If it is the latest "in" thing, Mother won't see her daughter left outside. With entry into junior high school, the ritual of pairing off and going steady begins in earnest, at least for the members of the more hip, "with-it," crowd. This raises pressures and a very real conflict for junior high school age boys. As every man can remember, that period of early adolescence is a time of miserable awkwardness for a boy. Often the girls in his class are taller than he is. The girls are at ease on a dance floor (at least they seem at ease) while he is still trying to keep from falling on his face. And in the interactions of boy-girl games, the girls in general are about three or four years ahead of the boys. The span is further increased if the dances, mixed parties, and dating are encouraged and/or permitted by parents. Boys who might still prefer riding bikes and shooting baskets on the playground now find themselves in a bind. Although the boy-girl games may not hold much appeal for them, they may feel compelled to go along with them in order not to risk being seen as still a "little kid." What we have, in effect, is a chain reaction of parents prodding daughters to plunge into the world of adult sexual-social relationships and drag the boys, however reluctantly, in with them.

And with what result? Children who are exposed to experiences and relationships long before they are ready to assume the necessary responsibility for them. And here, incidentally, lies a further irony: The mothers who often appear the most eager to push their twelve-year-old daughters into the social scene of playing the seductive role, going steady, and the rest are the very ones who bury their heads in the sand and refuse to consider even the possibility that with the door wide open, their sexy little girl may step all the way through and end up a thirteen-year-old mother!

No parent today can hope to hold back the tide, let alone turn the calendar back fifteen or twenty years. We are not living in the days of middy blouses, no lipstick in high school, and sweet-sixteen-and-never-been-kissed. But parents can draw lines and hold them if they are willing to pay the price of assuming the responsibility and authority of being parents. Which today means: Not going along with the crowd of *conformity-and-popularity-at-any-price* parents. In a culture in which we are bombarded from all sides to "be the first on your block" in literally everything, this is by no means an easy position to maintain. But it is a necessary stance since one cannot rely on the moderation and good sense of other parents. If we must "give way" to the trends of the times, and to a degree there is little choice but to do so (otherwise, we would run the risk of locking our children in an unreal world of the past), we can at least let the reins out slowly. Furthermore, we can stand firm in matters which we consider—by our values—to be truly important.

To cite one example: When mini-skirts first broke into fashion, some of the girls in both high school and junior high rushed to shorten their skirts. We didn't ask our daughters to be the last in school to raise their hemlines, but they were not going to be first with the highest. As shorter skirts became the accepted fashion among the great majority, they followed suit, but at a moderate rate. And never at the cost of what we (taking into consideration the changing fashions) would consider good taste. It had little or nothing to do with what used to be spoken of as "modesty." If topless bathing suits ever become the accepted female beachwear, we will have no objection to our daughters going topless. It has more to do with how fast we are going to let them or encourage them to communicate by their dress and behavior a sexual role which is beyond their level of maturity. Mini-skirts, we admit, are perhaps a poor example, so let's take another in which there has been a firmer line drawn—and held: going steady. And here we must define our terms and the ages at which our various rules apply. Going steady might be defined as dating the same boy or girl to the exclusion of all others, with or without any agreement or statement of commitment to one another and no others. By high school, this constitutes the majority of dating patterns. Fewer and fewer high school age boys and girls attempt to "play the field." Parents who try to convince them how much more fun they can have going out with different ones rather than being "tied down" are wasting their breath. In many high schools it is virtually a matter of go steady or don't date at all. There is another meaning which could be given to going steady: A very close relationship in which the boy and girl spend time together and behave toward one another in a way very similar to what we might expect of an engaged couple. They are together generally every afternoon after school, at her home, his home, or elsewhere, and often all afternoon and perhaps evening as well. These patterns of "going steady" have become increasingly prevalent even in the early teens. One of the things which strikes the observer in watching such young couples is the ease with which they seem to relate to each other. There is no awkwardness or tenseness. They are comfortable when together, able to express their thoughts and feelings with remarkable freedom. Constant exposure to one another breaks down the social barriers of unfamiliarity which initially exist between the sexes at that age. All too often, it breaks down other barriers as well. To expect that such a young couple will not engage in sexual relations is simply unrealistic. To state it like it is, it simply comes down to this: The teen-agers who are going steady by this latter definition had better have a prescription for the Pill or be willing to accept a pregnancy. And their parents better be prepared as well.

Here, as in other matters, we draw the line. To the mother who says, "Not my little girl. I've taught her right from wrong and I know she wouldn't do anything like that," we ask, "Is your daughter normal? If so, why do you expect other than a normal response?" Regardless of any teachings to the contrary, parents cannot expect children placed in situations of such close intimacy to not give in to the demands of a very powerful drive. There is an appalling lack of reality on the part of many parents when it comes to this matter. They wouldn't dream of putting their fifteen-year-old son behind the wheel of a powerful sports car and send him off on his own, confident that he won't speed "because we have taught him the rules of safety." Yet the temptation to drive fast is not likely to be as strong as the sexual temptations he will encounter spending every day with his steady girl friend.

You are not going to raise your daughters in a cloister or walk your sons back and forth to school each day. You want them to grow into healthy outgoing adults, not withdrawn neurotics. This means taking some risks. They may make mistakes. Their parents did, and still do. Supervision in the area of sexual activity means, for the most part, not placing the child in environments in which he or she will be facing adult choices when they are not yet ready for adult responsibility. As parents, you can never carry this all the way. Very few sixteen-year-olds are ready for the responsibilities of pregnancy, but few parents feel it would be healthy to forbid dating at sixteen. Not in *our* society. It is always a matter of "how much and how soon." Child rearing entails a gradual lessening of control and an increase in freedom and privileges. It is always hard to turn the process in reverse. Allow a certain freedom when the child is thirteen, and you may find yourself facing open revolt if you try taking away that freedom when he or she reaches fifteen.

In the following, we have attempted to give, in a very general outline, the freedoms and privileges as well as limits which are appropriate with each successive year of adolescence. By "appropriate" we mean "realistically considering the level of emotional maturity of the average child of that age." Parents may feel that their child is less mature than the average and may, therefore, decide to hold back a bit more. To permit the child to move ahead in the belief that he or she is more mature than the average at that age is a risk that hardly seems warranted. An error in the direction of conservatism seldom results in consequences as drastic as an error in the other direction.

Twelve–Thirteen (seventh–eighth grades): Beginning of boy friend-girl friend relationships may be permitted if parents have no reason for disapproving of the friend, but time and activities together are very limited. They are restricted to walking home from school together (but not elsewhere) and occasional visits to the house—under parental supervision at all times. No mixed parties at homes. School dances without dates—with parents providing transportation and with a "no leaving the hall" adequately enforced—is permissible. Slumber parties for girls are very big at this age. They can sometimes present a problem. They should be limited to those the parents can be sure are supervised by responsible parents (some slumber parties offer an opportunity for late-night meetings with boys). At this age, there is no justification for unsupervised dating—even in groups. Dating is an adult activity calling for adult roles and while no sensible parent today would lay down a no-dating rule for a sixteen- or seventeen-year-old, to permit it at twelve or thirteen is to push the child into a role for which the child is not yet prepared.

This can be a trying age for both parent and child. Even the name junior *high school* tends to imply a more mature role for the students than is warranted by age and experience. The twelve- and thirteen-year-old, especially if a girl, finds that first introduction to being "grownup" a very heady perfume. The rapidly changing figure, the onset of menstruation, the classmates with heavy make-up and sophisticated dress and hair styles are all introductions to the adult sexual role. The child should be led into this world. Too many adults are *throwing* children into it. It is well to keep in mind that the peer group influence, always strong throughout adolescence, is particularly powerful at this age. If parents lose the reins at this point, they may never regain them. The rule for parents should be: Keep the control, be *present*, and supervise.

Fourteen–Fifteen (ninth–tenth grades): Supervision of activities becomes more of a problem (or challenge) when the child enters high school, even if you live in a small town with a very small high school. For one thing, there are more activities available: field trips, club outings, football games, dances, etc., all school sponsored, plus a number of non-curricular, non-school affiliated activities. For another, supervision by adults in these activities tends to drop off—often to zero! At this point, parents may really feel they are fighting back a social tidal wave. All around, there are parents who seem to feel that beginning with high school all limits should come off, that ninth or tenth grade is the time for the child to start "doing his own thing." Until, of course, their offspring gets in trouble. The fight to keep some modicum of parental control worsens when the children are backed up by permissive teachers and counselors (who are not going to have to live with the problems after the child is picked up by the police for drugs or faces an unwed pregnancy), who harp on "The child can't be held down forever; they have to be free to make their own decisions." Of course, freedoms, privileges—*and responsibilities*—increase with each year, but there is no magic in any particular age or grade in school which transforms the child into the adult. High school covers four years of a child's adolescent years (in some areas, ninth grade is part of junior high). The entering freshman, perhaps thirteen years old, is suddenly caught up in an environment of student-driven automobiles and eighteen-year-old seniors sharing a table in the student lounge. But there is a long, long way from thirteen to eighteen. And the rights and privileges of the eighteen-year-old should be a mighty step from the rights and privileges of the thirteen- (or fourteen- or fifteen-) year-old. We say *should* be. Unless parents have a very firm hand on the reins from the start of those high school years, they won't be. The freshman will be doing the same things and with the same degree of freedom as the senior. When that happens, trouble is almost inevitable.

The freshman girl who manages to attract the attentions of a senior boy is understandably flattered, perhaps even awed. After all, doesn't it prove she looks and acts "mature for her age" if an older boy is interested in her (and more than a few mothers would eat that up). What she doesn't know (but her mother should) is that the freshman or sophomore girl becomes desirable "game" for that very reason. The seventeen- or eighteen-year-old boy has an advantage. He can come on like the big man on campus, the sophisticate, and chances are he is a bit more sophisticated than the easily flattered girl just beginning to learn her way around campus. The line that goes "You're not still a scared little kid, are you?" may be an old one, but don't think it no longer works. The fourteen- or fifteen-year-old boy or girl is *not* prepared to assume the responsibilities (and risks!) of a close boy-girl relationship. Parents should still, therefore, draw the line on the *day-by-day-always-together* going steady. This is the age at which dating should *begin*. And that sort of going steady isn't a beginning, it's almost an *end*. "Dating" will probably begin at this age (on a one-to-one basis), but common sense dictates that the parents set close limits on where and when. We find a good rule of thumb to follow at this age is to limit any dates to very special occasions such as the Freshman Ball, the Christmas Formal, etc. But not to a movie, beach party, or "informal" dance. This may strike some parents (and perhaps most teen-agers) as a rule wholly out of keeping with the 1970s. And it is, if we are to talk of what the tribal mores may be today. But it is based upon what we have stressed before; letting the reins out slowly enough so that by the time the child reaches sixteen, you still have something more to "give." Why the "formal" occasions? Two reasons: They provide a better opportunity for the boy or girl to learn the correct social roles of adult dating (what used to be called, in a bygone day, *etiquette*), and they provide an environment which is perhaps a little less emotionally "free." (The latter is somewhat difficult to explain briefly. We might put it this way: At this age, a boy and girl will probably be somewhat more inhibited in their overall behavior when dressed in formal attire.)

Activities in which transportation is provided by other high school (or college) age kids driving should, except in unusual circumstances, not be permitted. The freshman or sophomore is not yet old enough to be licensed to

drive, and going with an "older crowd" is, as we have
said, a risky business. Even if we shut our eyes to the fact
that there are more babies conceived out of wedlock in
automobiles than in motel rooms, we can hardly ignore the
gruesome statistics on teen-age accidents. They will soon
enough be endangering life and limb on the highways. We
prefer that it not be rushed. There are enough things going on to give any concerned parents sleepless nights. Why
add that one before it is time?

Just about everything we said about limits during the
junior high years should still apply—in general, that is.
There are more activities during high school and increased
maturity should carry with it increased freedoms, but this
is still an age calling for a good deal of parental and other
adult supervision. We still retain the right and authority
to say where they are going, with whom, and when they
are to be home. To almost all activities, we take them and
we pick them up. "Home right after school unless prior
permission obtained" is still a rule—and remains one all
through high school. And we still have the final say when
it comes to their dress and appearance. This may sound
repressive to some "modern" thinking (?) parents. It isn't.
And it doesn't result in rebellion. So long as the rules are
rational, the parents are genuinely concerned, the rules
are applied consistently and fairly, and above all, the family environment is one of warmth, love, and mutual respect, the children will respond with acceptance and
maturity.

Sixteen–Seventeen (eleventh–twelfth grades): The conclusion of high school should mark the end of the parents'
child-rearing obligations. From then on, the responsibilities and decisions should rest squarely on the shoulders of
the boy or girl. To stay at home or to leave. To go on to
college or to pass it up. To marry or not. To have sex before marriage. To hitchhike around the world. Or to join
the Mexican Navy. Whatever, the choice should now rest
with the son or daughter, not the parents.

The obligations should end because the overall authority ends. With high school completed, the child is no longer obliged to live at home, go to school, or in other ways remain under the jurisdiction of the parents. And if Johnny no longer is obligated to submit to parental rule, his parents cannot be expected to continue to assume responsibility for him.

The ways in which this works out in practice, however, frequently lead to confusion all around. Often, there is even a sort of reverse order to things. Johnny's parents permit him a no-holds-barred freedom while he is still in high school, only to follow him from one end of the earth to the other trying, by everything from persuasion to psychological warfare, to impose restrictions on his choices after he is out of school.

This doesn't mean we advocate throwing children out the door before the ink is dry on their high school diplomas. Or that we wash our hands of our children. *However,* at some point, the authority of parents must end. Completion of high school seems a logical time.

We do not believe parents have any *obligation*—legally or morally—to send children to college, despite what some teachers may feel or the practices of the parents' friends and neighbors. Nor do we feel the children are obliged to go. Today, the majority of middle-class children are deciding to continue their education beyond high school. It may be questioned whether many of these high school graduates will benefit from college, but that is another matter. The parents may rationally recognize they have no obligation to send their son or daughter to college, yet feel they would like to help the child pursue a higher education. Fine. But the child should understand that his parents are under no obligation to do so. And that whatever help they give is strictly a *gift.*

The sexual and social behavior of the child becomes increasingly a matter of the child's responsibility as he or she nears this point of "emancipation." When he is "on his own," the parents have no legitimate say in what he does or with whom he does it. To place it in reality: Your daughter may decide to go off to live with her boy friend in a mountain cabin a month after she finishes high school. You may not approve of her choice, but is there anything you can do to stop her? Of course not.

If you have a son or daughter still living at home while working or going to college, he still comes under some of the rules of the household just as every other member of the family (including the father and mother) does. No member of a household can be totally free to come and go as he pleases, assuming no responsibility toward the other members. If the daughter wants to move her boy friend into her bedroom while still living at home, the parents have every right to say yes or no. They still have authority in their home. After all, if you can lay down rules for someone boarding in your home, you can do so for one of your older children still living there. And this includes the hours that are kept and the activities which go on while at home. Let's face it: The child always has the choice at that age of moving out.

During that last couple of years of high school, however, you as parents still hold both the responsibility and the authority. More frequent boy-girl activities will be permitted. Single dating on both a formal and informal basis will probably increase to frequency of once a week, perhaps twice. And "going steady" will become a much more *steady* relationship. Many activities which might not have been permitted a year before will now be given parental sanction. Yet this should not mean that the parental reins are cut during those two years, or even the last semester of the senior year. Increasing privileges should never be taken as a sign that "anything goes." And, assuming the parents have kept control up to this time, they won't.

Now, however, is a time for the parents, as well as the child, to face squarely the reality of the situation that soon the child will make *all* of the important decisions which the parents have, in whole or in part, made for the child for all these years. If the parents have done a conscientious job of child rearing, they can expect that the child's future decisions will be responsible ones. But the human being still has freedom of choice, and no parent can ensure a child against irresponsibility or folly.

When your teen-age son or daughter goes out on a date, you cannot (by any reasonable means) ensure that he or she will not engage in sexual relations any more than you can prevent them from smoking pot. Moral guidance, lectures, warnings, and whatever go just so far. Then it is up to the individual.

There is one thing you can do, however. You can make sure they have the full range of choices available to them, including the choice of a reliable contraceptive should they decide to have sexual relations. Such a suggestion might come as a shock to some parents. Twenty years ago, it would have been sure to. But this isn't twenty years ago, or even ten. And reality is reality. Parents may feel that the answer lies in self-control, but the answer for whom? In this most imperfect world, the "perfect" answers of some parents simply deny reality.

The reality *is* clear: First, there is a probability that your son or daughter will engage in premarital sexual intercourse regardless of what teaching you may attempt to instill. Second, pregnancy which might result would find two kids who are almost totally unprepared for the responsibilities of parenthood. The harshness of such realities does nothing to dispel their existence. They are simply facts to be faced by parents in these times. Doesn't it make sense, therefore, to prepare the child by making available to him or her the means to prevent—with some sureness—conception?

This can start with a talk about contraceptives. In the better sex education courses in the high schools, contraceptive information is given, but don't rely on the course. Your child may not have gotten it or may still have unanswered questions. (Make sure, of course, that *you* have the facts!) There are a number of contraceptive methods, but when speaking of the unmarried teen-ager, practical considerations limit the choices. Vaginal foams, supposi-

tories, and the like are simply not practical under the circumstances in which the boy and girl will be likely to have
relations. The vaginal diaphragm is not suitable for use by
a teen-age girl, and the condom isn't sure enough. There
are, at present, only two methods which approach 100
per cent: the Pill and the intra-uterine device (IUD).
There is now an IUD available which shows promise of
being able to be employed with women who have not
previously given birth, but it is still doubtful a doctor
would recommend the device for a young girl. That leaves
only the Pill as a sure method of birth control which can
be employed with practicality by the unmarried teen-ager.

The sixteen-year-old boy can walk into the drugstore
and purchase condoms, even though they may not be
the surest. But few doctors would prescribe the Pill for a
teen-age girl still living at home without consent of the
parents. This, of course, puts the girl in quite a spot. It
would take considerable courage for most young girls to
come to Mom and Dad and ask permission to get a prescription for the Pill even if she might anticipate a favor-
able response. Nor would she be any more apt to go in to
see the doctor if she knew he would call her parents. It
simply calls for too much of an admission, too much a re-
linquishment of her privacy. There is a way the situation
can be handled, however, if the parents are willing to
face up to it with maturity and understanding. The parents can provide the doctor with written permission *in advance,* which will allow him to prescribe the Pill if their
daughter should decide to seek his help. They may then
talk with their daughter and explain what they have done.
How the parents handle such a conversation is important.
It should not communicate, "We know you're going to
do it, so you better play it safe." You *don't* know that she
will, and to put it that way makes it an accusation and a
statement of your opinion of her. It can be explained that
you have confidence in her ability to make responsible
decisions, that you trust her judgment in this matter as
in others, but that from your own experience you realize

fully that sexual desire can be very strong; her mother and father experience the same feelings. She can be told that *if* she should decide at any time in the future to engage in sexual relations, she can and should take steps to ensure against an unwanted pregnancy, and that she can make an appointment with the doctor and obtain a prescription without your ever knowing. It should be a conversation which communicates your love and concern, your acceptance of realities and your respect for your daughter.*

* Much more could be said concerning the problems of sexual behavior during these years of adolescence. For a very sane approach to the problems, we strongly recommend parents read *Sex Before Marriage,* a highly readable book authored by Eleanor Hamilton, Ph.D. (Bantam Books, 1969). And after reading it, give it to your teen-ager.

11

THE FAMILY TOGETHER
—AND OTHERS

Since adults choose to have children, one might expect them to enjoy them. Yet all we observe leads us to conclude otherwise. Families have all but lost their ability to find enjoyment in each other. Many don't even try. Father goes his way to the golf course, a hunting trip, or television. Mother goes her way to coffee klatches, bridge parties, or involvement in a "cause." And the children move from one diversion to another, some supervised, some not.

The so-called "nuclear family" has exploded in all directions; like a shattered atom, the members leave the center with ever increasing speed. Can we really believe, then, the human beings who make up this nominal family truly enjoy one another?

Perhaps they might, if they spent enough time together to really get to know one another. But then, many things might be rewarding if we would but make the investment in time and effort to develop them. The price of being a *family* today is high, and getting higher. Everything we have discussed in the preceding chapters has involved a price, the price of raising children rationally in a society no longer noted for its rationality (if it ever was). One of the major prices is the same each time: the struggle of going counter to the mass of other families. Which is never easy. Many parents talk glowingly of the value of family unity and "togetherness," yet enroll their children in scouting, send them off to camp during the summer, and sign them up for every "outside" children's activity that comes along. What we will cover in this chapter pits both parent and child against the prevailing mores as much as anything we have covered.

First, however, it might be worthwhile to consider what is to be gained by developing a family which can "play together." The benefits accrue to parents as well as children. Parents can learn to enjoy their children; children can learn to enjoy their parents; and children can be raised with the values the parents hold to be important. The closer your family is able to work and play together, the more you, the parents, can expect to exert a positive influence in the development of your children. Children tend to respect the opinions of adults whose company they enjoy. It's as simple as that. Parents also can find an additional benefit. Some of the best opportunities to know and understand the child are provided by those times when parents and children are having fun together.

Children *can* be fun, despite what we see of monstrous little brats screaming in department stores and upsetting glasses of milk in restaurants. Needless to say, however, the fun times don't just happen. They have to be built on a foundation of discipline and planned with an application of very uncommon common sense. Most parents manage to have fun with their children from time to time, but it becomes somewhat like playing a roulette wheel. If they are lucky, they have a good day, or it may start out as a good day and end up chaotic, or the whole day may fall apart right from the start. Since children are supposed to be unpredictable, you can't really be sure any activity will turn out to be a joyous occasion for all, right? Not quite. Life has its uncertainties, but by eliminating the most common mistakes, parents can load things in favor of a happy outcome each and every time. And as they gain experience, the odds increase in their favor. So let's first look at those common mistakes.

1. *Activities are planned without a realistic assessment of the interests of the child at that age.* The eight-year-old doesn't have the same interests at play as the four-

year-old or twelve-year-old. Knowing the child and his interests at that age becomes an important first step in the planning.

2. *Activities are planned for children of one age and ignore the interests of children of other ages in the family.* With an age spread of several years among the children of a family, it can be a distinct challenge to plan activities enjoyable to all (including the parents). Frequently, parents will either plan an activity suitable to the younger child to the frustration of the older children or select an activity for the older ones and bore the younger ones. In time, they may resort to leaving one or another home from planned activities and try to solve the dilemma by "taking turns." With that, there is a further split in the family unit. Activities can be planned which will meet the interests of all members; later, we will discuss some possibilities.

3. *A lack of coordination of the roles of Father and Mother in the planned activity.* One parent can ordinarily plan and supervise a family activity with considerable success (if not ease) if it is necessary, but when both parents go along on the activity and the roles of each are unclear or one of them (often the father) plays little part in the planning and supervision, things can break down.

4. *Timing is not given sufficient consideration.* When is as important as *what*, in the planning of most family activities. As we all know, young children tire quickly. If the parents are too late in going or stay until after the children have reached their limit, the day may end with nerve-shattering unpleasantness.

5. *Too much is planned for one day.* Young children are especially susceptible to overstimulation. If too much is included in the day's activities, they may tire rapidly, become hyperactive, and dissolve in temper or tears. Seeing all the sights at Disneyland in one day with a six-year-old is an almost sure way to unglue both parents and child.

6. *Dress is inappropriate for the activities.* This usually results from scheduling two or more very different ac-

tivities the same day, e.g., going to the park following church on Sunday; the children are dressed up for church in their best clothes so the parents don't feel they can be permitted to go down the slide and climb trees at the park. The dress should be appropriate to all activities planned for the day in order to avoid frustration—on the part of parents as well as children.

7. *Plans are revealed too soon.* The best-made plans of parents must sometimes be changed or dropped. If the child has been promised a trip to the zoo on the weekend, and the trip must be called off, the weekend may be overshadowed with gloom. Family activities should seldom, if ever, be used as promised rewards (which is the usual reason for revealing the plans in advance). Furthermore, plans revealed far in advance can turn a child's thoughts to little else. The child who is told on Monday that parents plan a day at the circus for Saturday may think of nothing else for the week; it can then be a reward which backfires.

8. *Not planning the expenses realistically.* If the activity is going to take money, the expenditures should be anticipated beforehand. A realistic budget should be set in order to avoid last-minute cancellation of plans or undue strain. This is especially important in planning activities such as trips to an amusement park where expenses for the day can vary widely.

9. *Including other adults in the activity.* Inviting adult friends or relatives on a family outing or "double-dating" with other parents and their children is seldom wise. The adults end up talking together. The parents and children are not together as a family unit. And there is little chance that two families, when brought together for the day, will move at the same pace or pursue the same interests in similar ways. The necessary compromises often lessen the harmony desired in a family activity.

10. *Lack of participation by parents in the activity.* Children most enjoy it when their parents take part in the planned activity rather than merely providing it for

the children and standing by as observers. Parents also have more fun if they do more than just take the children to the beach, park, zoo, or amusement center. Passive "baby-sitting" isn't much fun for parents *or* children. Joining in with the children can reduce both the generation gap and any undesired image of martyred parents.

The Family Day.   With the various demands of job, school, friends, and what-have-you, it isn't always easy to even assemble all family members in any one place at one time. Willie is off with friends at the school playground. Mary is over at a friend's house. Dad went down to the hardware store and Mom is having coffee with a neighbor. At times it seems the members of families in our complex society pass one another like strangers on a crowded avenue.

The *Family Day* can provide something of an answer to the problem, at least one day a week. It is one day each week, usually on the weekend when the parents are not working, set aside for family activities. In our family, it's Sunday, but the day obviously isn't important. What is important is that the same day each week be reserved strictly for the family. No friends dropping in. No permissions to go off separately. Activities, whatever they may be, planned to include all members of the family.

That key word: planning! As we all know, it is all too easy to let weekends slip by. Unless plans have been made ahead of time, parents find themselves caught up in household chores, television watching, or doing "not much of anything." Saturdays can go by with the children glued to the television or playing with friends only to announce Sunday morning that they have homework assignments which will occupy all that day. Mother may discover a week's ironing which simply must be done. And the man of the house may have promised a friend to help build a patio. It is best if the parents make their plans for the day several days in advance so when family day arrives they are ready to "get moving." If they wait until that morning, there is a better than even chance the last-minute plans won't be entirely satisfactory. The important thing is that all members know that family day is held "sacred," that it is the one day of the week reserved for family activities—no exceptions.

Family day does not mean you must go somewhere each time. A lot of fun is to be had at home. But both take planning.

The family day outing: Many parents are like the typical husband. When it comes to where to go on a day or an evening out, imagination is not his long suit. The same activities are repeated with what can become monotonous frequency. Even very "special" and expensive outings can be repeated to the point of boredom. We know one set of parents in southern California who took their family to Disneyland (close to two hundred miles round trip) every weekend for almost a year! That, we submit, should be enough to turn any child into Mickey Mouse or a raving maniac. In even a rural community far from any "active" centers, there are a number of places to go and things to see, many of which don't cost much: parks, lakes, band concerts, community theatre, school museums. If you live near a city, even a moderate-sized one, try writing to the chamber of commerce for information on places of interest. Even long-time residents are often unaware of all their community has to offer. Keep in mind the sort of things which can provide entertainment for children. Earth-moving equipment on a road construction, a tour through a fire station, or for the child of the city, a visit to a farm or a dairy can offer education as well as a lot of fun. Time spent by parents in planning the outings with imagination can also keep family days from becoming dull for Father and Mother.

Follow a schedule in your outings. In planning and carrying through a successful day out with young children, timing is important. Traveling can be tiring to little ones so a general rule to follow is: On any outing involving a lengthy drive, leave early and return early. Try to have

some plan of where and when you will eat. Many a day
has been spoiled by arriving at the destination just about
nap time or by pushing the activities beyond the hunger
point. If you know it's going to be a long day with a late
arrival home, throw some pillows in the back of the car;
they just may sleep all the way home. Feeding the family
on all-day outings does not have to be the problem so
many families make it. "Snacking" throughout the day on
hot dogs, soft drinks, ice cream, can be asking for trouble
with small ones. And it can be expensive. Even a sack of
popcorn and a soft drink for each member of the family
including Mom and Dad can run into money at today's
prices and what have you? At most ball parks and zoos,
however, there is nothing says Mom can't make popcorn
at home and supply each member with his own sack.
Roadside or station wagon tailgate picnics can usually fill
the bill for all-day outings. They are fun; they save the
time it takes to eat in a restaurant and they help with the
money control. Provided they are kept within limits, they
are very little fuss to prepare. Certainly they don't need
to be the old-fashioned picnic with tables spread with an
awesome variety of hot and cold dishes resembling a farm
dinner for a crew of thrashers. A stack of peanut butter
and jelly sandwiches, some fruit, and a thermos of something cool to drink should do it. The whole lunch can fit
in one box, and with a damp washrag brought along in a
plastic bag, it can be a quick, almost effortless, affair.

Should you decide to take the family to a restaurant,
some preliminary groundwork can keep it from becoming
the ulcer-producing episode so many parents find it. Here
are a few suggestions: Make the bathroom stop before going to the restaurant. A stop at a service station to take care
of the clean-up and "etc." avoids the sometimes troublesome trips through a crowded maze of tables. Decide,
before you enter the restaurant, what sort of meal you
plan. In most cases, the parents can have the order in mind
ahead of time and can avoid lengthy discussions and requests when the waitress hands a menu to each child.

Your teen-agers and preteens may order from the menu, but the parents can set the limits before. Drinks usually add an unnecessary amount to the luncheon tab and increase the later comfort stops. Since water is served, you can say no to the soft drinks and milk. A short briefing session in the car before you go in to eat is a big help in maintaining control. Children, especially younger ones, need reminding. Go over the rules of restaurant behavior —and the penalty for any infraction. One rule we have found helpful: Hands are to be kept in the lap until food is served: no reaching for glasses of water, etc. Parents are to decide on the order for the younger ones—with no arguments permitted. Voices are to be kept down, and no complaints allowed. With the parents keeping a firm hand on an "or else" basis, they can escape the feeling of "let's eat in a hurry and get out of here before something happens."

Keeping voices down should also be the rule while on the road. Probably no one knows how many accidents have been caused by parents rattled by high-pitched children's voices, to say nothing of the tension headaches. Children *can* be taught to sit quietly and talk softly. And there is nothing to prevent a parent from stopping along the side of the road to administer a firm spanking. If order is to be kept, however, the children can't be ignored. If Dad is engrossed in the ball game on the car radio or the parents are excluding the children from their conversation, things can quickly get out of line. Drawing them into the conversation, pointing out sights along the way, talking about what you are going to see or their impressions of what they saw, can frequently keep the lid on things, reduce teasing, bickering, complaints, and requests.

If the activities can call for more expenditures than just a single admission charge, establish what you plan to do ahead of time. Nothing is more unpleasant than constant requests for balloons, rides, souvenirs, and the rest. You can let the children know beforehand they are not to ask for anything—just wait until it's offered. Don't let them come to expect something additional each time. A trip to the zoo does not have to be coupled with balloons that pop or snow cones which make a mess. At carnivals and amusement parks, we find it easiest when the children are old enough to start handling money to give each one a set amount to spend with the understanding that that's it; when it's gone, no more pleading.

Try to plan activities which will offer something to each member of the family, including the parents. This isn't as hard as it may seem. Unless the children have been raised with the example of a mother who won't go to football games with her husband "because I just don't like football" or a father who "wouldn't be caught dead at a ballet," you should be able to come up with many activities which will prove fun for sixteen-year-olds as well as six-year-olds. We spent a summer touring Europe with our nine children when the eldest was sixteen and the youngest, six. We found no problem in planning days for the entire family. The sights at Hampton Court Palace our teen-agers found most fascinating were not those which turned on the younger ones, but the day was no less memorable. Not long ago we read a newspaper series written by the parents of several children recounting their adventures traveling with their children through Europe. It read like the *Perils of Pauline*. It didn't tell us much about travel in Europe, but it did tell us a lot about a very disorganized family. In a book on travel with children, the author advised against taking children of six or seven (or presumably younger) on long air trips. "You can't expect them to sit still, and the running up and down the aisles will drive you and the other passengers crazy." "If you plan to take the children to Europe, do it before they reach their teens; when they get older, they won't want to go places with the family." Another rather sad exposure of the author's family experience. Of course, young children can be taught to sit quietly on an airplane. And if the members of the family have learned to have fun together, why should the teen-agers not want to be included?

Obviously, in selecting the activity you give thought to the interests of the family members, and to the interest level and boredom levels. A four-hour visit to an art museum will probably prove too much for a six-year-old. If the teen-agers have not become too "sophisticated," they should still enjoy a trip to the zoo or the rides at an amusement park (if they do feel they are too "grownup," perhaps it is time for some parent-child discussions on the meaning of maturity and responsibility).

One further bit of advice on outings: Try to have one or two alternate plans in mind in event changes in the weather or other unforeseen events make your primary plan inadvisable. If the outing is called off, be able to offer plans for a fun day at home. It takes out the sting of disappointment and keeps the day a "family day."

Family Day at Home. We *like* parties. Not the neurotic cocktail events where adults down liquid tranquilizers in order to be able to talk to one another. We like family parties. We don't need any special occasion. Oh sure, birthdays and holidays are observed with all the trimmings, but we also find other good reasons to plan parties. If we can't find a reason, we have a party anyway, family parties. Perhaps you could say we celebrate being together as a family and having fun. Who needs a better reason?

We have held champagne breakfasts to celebrate an achievement by one of the children, getting-out-of-school parties, valentine parties, St. Nicholas' Day parties, Easter vacation parties, birthday parties, Junior High graduation parties, and "just because it's a good day" parties. You see what we mean when we say we like parties?

We try to give the family day at home something of the flavor of a party. It should not, we feel, be simply a day in which everyone is expected to stay home, possibly with resentment. Family day should be the day in each week every family member looks forward to. Many activities can make it so. A game of Monopoly or cards, croquet, planting a family garden with the flower or vegetable choices left to each member, a picnic in the family room with hot dogs roasted in the fireplace, a backyard barbecue, even a family finger-painting party at the kitchen table can turn the family day into a day to be anticipated and remembered.

Most of all, family days should be times for sharing ideas and observations, opportunities to be close. What is done is not so important. The spirit in which it is done is. Even cooking the breakfast or evening meal together as a real family activity can prove to be something special. They should be relaxed days for everyone with a minimum of work for parents and children. The purpose of the family day is *play,* not work.

When it comes to guests on family days, we are restrictive. No adult guests. They invariably take the attention of the parents away from children. Other evenings, other days, we may invite friends, but on family day, the welcome mat for adults is definitely withdrawn. At times, permission is given for one of the children's friends to join us on family day, but the emphasis stays with the family— and what we do together.

Parents as Teachers. Given sufficient time, books, and materials, most parents could do a more than adequate job of educating their children at home without ever sending them off to school. They might even do a better job than many of the schools are presently doing. Most parents, however, are not in a position to take on such a task even if they wanted to. And many parents would not feel qualified. They have been brainwashed into believing that teaching a child to read or to add and subtract calls for extensive education in teaching methods as well as the subject matter. (It doesn't!) If Mr. and Mrs. Jones did decide to tackle the job of educating their children at home, they would no doubt encounter massive resistance from others spouting psychological gobbledygook: "The child needs the social environment of the other children at school; around the neighborhood and with brothers and sisters isn't enough. They will develop all sorts of hang-ups, probably become introverts." In any case, the parents would undoubtedly be dragged into court. Deviation from the educational system is a punishable offense.

Much as we might like to, we may not be able to assume the entire teaching role, but if our children are going to gain an education which will prepare them to function rationally and purposefully, their most important education must come through us.

Like everything else in child rearing, this calls for involvement—and then some. Purchasing an encyclopedia and building a well-stocked library are fine, but no substitute for "individual instruction" by parents. This has become increasingly important, in fact imperative, in recent years as our schools have shifted philosophy and emphasis from learning to conforming, from self-discipline to self-indulgence, and from achievement to mediocrity in the name of equality. In schools staffed by losers and dedicated to turning out mass-produced, "well-adjusted" (to what?) losers, our children are being taught that achievement is an immoral discrimination against non-achievers, that self-interest is evil, and that honest inquiry is dangerous. How to combat their well-organized efforts to educationally lobotomize our children? Only one way: Children thirst for knowledge. They seek to expand, to grow. Provide an honest intellectual food at home and they will recognize the ersatz educational pablum for what it is.

Parents, regardless of their own formal education, possess a great deal of valuable knowledge about a lot of things. Sharing this knowledge, together with teaching how all the individual bits and pieces of information integrate in a mosaic of a rational and understandable picture of the world, is both a challenge and a deep satisfaction.

A family outing, a television documentary watched and discussed by the family, or the planting of a back-yard vegetable garden can open up opportunities for expanding the children's knowledge of the world. On the outing, Father and Mother may point out any number of things of interest, sharing what information they may have with the children. We may introduce them to the wonders of geology, prompted by a view of the hills, or the workings of diesel motors, prompted by a passing truck, or an explanation of how fish "breathe" through their gills when Junior lands his first one. We are not geologists, automotive experts, or marine biologists. And perhaps you aren't either. But we have picked up a lot of information here and there in the years we have lived. We can share this information as well as our experience. A TV news special, a travelogue, or a science feature can be a springboard for a family seminar. The program material can be expanded upon and can provide impetus for further reading and exploration in the area. A vegetable garden can be an instructional laboratory for the study of a variety of plant and insect life. We don't have to be experts on everything if we are willing to take time to "look it up."

We have made great use of the evening dinner table as a free wheeling classroom. Children, even high schoolers, seldom, if ever, read a news magazine "from cover to cover." If we keep up with what is going on in the world (and we feel we should), we can draw on our information to fill in the gaps on the current state of the world. A free flow of conversation, we have found, always provides leads for informal "instruction," discussions of South American geography, space exploration, a recent medical discovery, the President's latest run-in with Congress, the population explosion, professional football, modern art, the function of our courts, women's liberation, the history of World War II, atomic energy, or what causes earthquakes. (A major bonus in raising children: We can learn a lot.)

There are also those "practical" skills we teach in the home. Actually, all education has a practical value; or at least it should have. That is, it should be goal directed. These practical skills, however, are those we all need in our day-to-day existence (unless, of course, we have a domestic staff, which we don't). They include cooking, housekeeping, yard maintenance, sewing, ironing, washing, home repairs, painting, automobile maintenance, and the dozen and one other things one needs to know in order to keep things—and one's life—running smoothly. Some of these subjects are offered in school, but the level at which they are taught would not, in most cases, adequately prepare a thirteen-year-old for baby-sitting. One mother told us of the final exam in her fifteen-year-old daughter's class in cooking: The students were to bake a cake—from a boxed mix! Even if the schools were to offer adequate courses, we feel these skills are best taught at home. First of all, it offers good opportunities for parent-child interaction on the level of family members working together; it helps teach family membership responsibility. Second, if the child is going to fulfill the academic requirements for further education beyond high school, he will probably not have time in his schedule for these electives. And third, it can be a lot of fun!

Boys can learn to cook as well as girls, and they should. Girls can be taught to change fuses and tires as capably as their brothers. And why not? As we said before, the day of sex role stereotyping is at an end. And if we raise our children with an adequate education, our sons will be skilled at cooking every bit as much as they are at unplugging a clogged drain. And so will their sisters.

"Extracurricular" Education. What a couple of decades ago might have been thought of as an upper-class affectation and a status symbol for upwardly mobile parents has become "a necessary part of the child's education": music lessons, dancing lessons, riding lessons, art lessons, and karate lessons. As part of the child's education, however, these hold a position quite different from mathematics, history, or literature. For one thing, they are most often initiated at the request (pestering?) of the child. His friends are playing musical instruments and he wants to join in the fun. He launches a campaign for a guitar (today's first choice) or a drum or clarinet, and his

parents, after considering the lesser of musical evils, noise levels, and cost, start him on music lessons.

Here, another difference often shows up. Developing skill on a musical instrument calls for as much work as developing skill in a foreign language. And not necessarily any more fun. "Playing" an instrument, once a skill has been developed, may be a lot of fun. But practice on the instrument is plain work, both tedious and boring. If enough skill is ever developed to make playing enjoyable, a great deal of practice time will have gone into it. Before that point is reached, he may lose interest. He probably will. He grows weary of going over and over those scales and exercises. So often, when the child reaches that stage, the parents give in and let him drop the lessons. They may feel he lacks any "natural talent," overlooking the fact that talent, like genius, is 10 per cent inspiration and 90 per cent perspiration. Young Willie may never become a second Wagner, but then, he may never become a second Einstein, yet we wouldn't think of letting him drop mathematics after only a few months. If the guitar is to be strictly for fun, then we should view it as we would any other toy (albeit an expensive toy). If we see it as part of his total education, we should supervise the education and set the goals. If we want children to "get an exposure" to music or dancing or whatever, we may decide on two years (minimum) of lessons and a half hour daily practice as a realistic "exposure." A complete education would demand much more. That decision belongs to the parents. Certainly, we want to carefully consider the feelings and desires of our children, and hopefully we will not enroll them in dancing lessons, riding class, or anything else in order to meet our status need. When all is said and done, however, it is up to the parents to decide. And it is our responsibility to see to it the program is followed.

Activities with Others. The world is a social world. We cannot shut people out of it, and we cannot shut people away from our children. The world may be populated by slightly mad people, but we cannot lock our children away from them. So long as they are still dependent on their parents and living with us as members of our family, our responsibility, however, includes some say about their involvement in activities outside the family. In Chapter 9 we discussed some of the steps parents can take in dealing with undesirable playmates and friends—and a lot *can* be done. Involvement in organized activities is something else. And often more of a challenge to parents.

What we will say will be generalizations, and generalizations, as everyone knows, are dangerous. And very much open to attack. We don't intend to modify them, but we will qualify enough to say that they apply to families in which both parents are *concerned* and *involved*, willing to assume the full responsibility of parenthood.

That said, we are willing to generalize. We find little of value in the adult-directed and adult-sponsored youth groups which have become almost sacred institutions in contemporary society. This includes scouting (and similar organizations for both boys and girls), Little League (including Pony League, Legion baseball, etc.), church youth groups, and a rather large number of other organizations for children. We realize this is even worse than attacking motherhood and the flag, but such institutions have become so much a part of the life of children, they can neither be ignored nor placed above critical examination.

Any of these involvements should be judged within the framework of the overall goals we, as the parents, hold for the rearing of our children, what we want them to learn, what influences we wish them exposed to. Every one of these adult-sponsored and supervised organizations is praised for its educational value. They teach good sportsmanship, camping skills, religion, baseball, handicrafts, and/or a set of seemingly desirable social loyalties and values. Can anyone object to that? Certainly not. But one might still question who is to do the teaching, and what else they may be teaching beyond the stated programs.

If you enjoy camping, you will probably anticipate tak-

ing the family camping, and they don't need membership
in Scouts to teach them what you are already teaching
them. If you hold religious convictions, you have family
religious practices which have probably been a part of the
overall education you have provided. Why send them
elsewhere to learn the religion you profess?

Each of these organizations provides surrogate parenthood. This may, in fact, be their appeal to parents, though
we doubt many parents are more than eager to turn over
child-raising responsibilities lock, stock, and barrel to the
schools. If some parents choose to turn over even more of
their parenthood to others, we will not argue with them.
But we refuse to join them. We are not willing to share our
parenthood with Little League coaches and Brownie leaders. And for two reasons: First, we enjoy our children. We
have fun with them. We have fun as a family. If we have
daughters in the Campfire Girls and sons in Indian Guides,
we are going to find those family times coming in second.
And we happen to feel there is good reason to keep the
family first. Second, as parents, we want to maintain some
say over who we turn our children over to and what their
influences and values may be.

The men and women leaders of the groups are individuals. They hold opinions and values just as you do. But
whether the Boy Scout leader holds views similar to yours
is another matter. Your values in the areas of family life,
education, religion, social and moral obligations, and a
host of others may vary greatly from his without their
meaning one or the other of you is "wrong" or "bad." It
does mean your views differ. And this is important.

The Little League coach and the church youth group
leader stand in the shoes of the parents—*in loco parentis.*
By implication at least, they express the values of the parents. These values may not be verbalized, but they can be
communicated as effectively through actions.

Suppose the Little League coach has an insecure self-
image and is seeking support for his faltering masculinity
through his role in athletics. Suppose further that he is us-

ing his coaching as a way to escape an intolerable home life.

Or perhaps the woman who leads the church youth group is bitter toward marriage and the role of women; frigid and anti-sexual.

Does any of this have anything to do with coaching baseball or teaching Bible lessons? Directly, perhaps no. Indirectly, it could be important. It is virtually impossible for any of us to keep our values hidden from those we work with day after day. We reveal them in many ways, our actions and reactions, chance remarks, expressions, and inflections. And the values of these surrogate parents will, in time, be communicated to the children. If the substitute parent holds the same values you do, your values are being reinforced. If not, whose values will your child adopt? Or will he just end up further confused?

Even if the adult could stick strictly on the subject matter, value judgments are involved. You may enjoy baseball and feel your son would enjoy it. To you it may be a game and you might hope your child would see it as only a game, a sport played for the fun of it. But what if that coach teaches a "win at any price" outlook, and more than a few such coaches do? You may want your children to grow up believing God is love and viewing their religion as a joyful part of their life. That leader of the church youth group may belong to your church but she may be steeped in a hell, brimstone, and damnation evangelism. What then?

One might, of course, argue that a similar conflict of values problem may exist from the time the child enters school. Not all teachers are going to hold the same convictions you do, and they have even more hours each week with your children. True enough. And no parent of school-age children can be unaware of the difficulties *that* can create. In most cases, however, it cannot be eliminated. The parents can attempt to counter some of the more outlandish ideas presented by the teacher (and children are very receptive to rationality; they quickly discover if

the teacher is stupid, crazy, or both), but short of taking
your family aboard a sailboat and cruising around the
world for a few years, there is no practical way to keep
them out of school and educating them yourself. You don't,
however, have to subject them to still more surrogate parental influence. Nothing says you must join the other
screaming parents berating their ten-year-olds from the
bleachers of a Little League ball park or send your daughter off to a Brownie leader who involves herself with other
women's children in order to escape the frustrations of her
own home.

The other familiar argument goes something like this:
"Since your children are going to have to live in this world,
is it right to try to shield them from all outside influence?"
First of all, we are not suggesting any such thing. But
none of us need worry on that score. Unless you are living
on a desert island with no passing ships, your children are
exposed to more possible influences today than ever before, thanks to television and a mass compulsion to become
"involved." We simply have a bias, and a strong one at
that: Since we hold the primary responsibility in raising
our children, we intend to do our best to remain the primary influence on their lives during those formative years.
In a society in which so many are "other-directed," parenthood has increasingly tended toward "child rearing by consensus." Parents are often desperately eager to share the
decisions with neighboring parents, school personnel, and
newspaper advice columnists. And how quickly the children learn of this insecurity. Nine-year-olds not only use
the argument "Jimmy and Billy get to do it; why can't
I?" they even suggest their parents call Jimmy's parents for
advice. Is it any wonder so many children are reaching
adulthood with confused uncertain values? And so many
hold the over-thirty generation in contempt?

A few years ago a national magazine ran a feature on
what they termed "untouchables," prominent public figures who were so revered they were treated by the press
as above any criticism whatsoever. Since then, some of

their "untouchables" such as J. Edgar Hoover and Jacqueline Kennedy Onassis may have fallen from the heights, but there can be no doubt we do bestow such protective mantles on a handful of personalities and institutions. Scouting, Campfire Girls, YMCA and YWCA, and church youth groups enjoy this protection by consensus. We are therefore well aware we risk an accusation of blasphemy in what we say. Even more, we risk misinterpretation, and for this reason, we wish to make the following points:

1. We are not making a value judgment—morally, ethically, or socially—on any individual involved in leading these youth groups. Most, we are sure, are persons of high principles who serve as excellent models for youth. At the same time, however, we are not unaware that the values and attitudes of the majority of adults in our society are at variance with ours. If they were not, we would be satisfied with the direction our society is taking in the education and guidance of children—and this book would not have been written. We can only assume, therefore, that the values of the majority of such leaders are representative of the values of the majority of other adults, values we are forced, all too often, to reject.

2. We have no desire to keep our children from the company and companionship of other children. As a matter of fact, we encourage them to invite their friends. Most of the time, it seems, we have as many of their friends at our home as we have children—which makes for a sizable crowd. No one would argue that children have no influence on other children, and thus the parents need not concern themselves with the children their offspring select as companions. Why should we not be concerned with the values held by adults who are potentially an even stronger influence? As parents, we do make judgments where our children's friends are concerned. If the influence is thought to be undesirable, we take steps. Why can't we also evaluate the values of these adult leaders? The answer in most cases is that the adult seldom reveals his or her values to another adult as clearly as a child does. What is re-

vealed to the parents on parents' night may be only the tip of the iceberg. We want to know the make-up of the entire iceberg. And this is often impossible. It might be easier to pass our responsibility to other surrogate parents, but what then? Do we resign our parenthood? Not on your life!—Or ours!—Or theirs!

One further gift we give our children, perhaps the most valuable: our relationship as a man and woman, their parents. Parenthood is a full-time job—for both parents. As a man and woman very much in love, we have a life of our own. We are not first Father and Mother; we are Joseph and Lois, the two of us, together. The closeness of our relationship is one of the most—and perhaps *the* most—important gifts we can ever hope to give our children. So long as they are dependent on us, however, they will be our responsibility, an all-inclusive one. We enjoy full-time parenthood. When it ends, it ends. Once they are on their own, our responsibilities end. We can then step out of their lives and go on with the love affair we have not relinquished during the years during which we have lived with them. If we have consistently assumed the full responsibility of our parenthood, we can do so with confidence and pride. Until that day, the reins will remain firmly in our hands. It has a lot to do with self-confidence. A lot to do with responsibility. And even more to do with loving.

12

SURVIVAL FOR THE SEVENTIES

Without an underlying set of principles, values, goals and aims, child rearing falls apart. It becomes a series of crisis interventions. And the lack of stability and consistency serves only to further confuse the child who is struggling to survive and grow in an ever confusing world.

If we attain our goals as parents, we will have taught our children an approach to life which will permit them not only to survive in the years ahead, but to grow. The following life values, then, are what we strive to give our children:

Reason and Rationality. The ability to approach the world, its challenges, and opportunities with reason is essential to happiness. Attainment of any satisfying life goals depends on rational thinking. Rational thinking, however, is not taught in our schools, seldom fostered by institutions, and rarely exhibited in our present society. Irrationality pervades so much of what is presented to our children, it is little wonder so many parents have difficulty understanding the values and attitudes their children bring home. If we don't teach them to think in a clear, logical way, they won't learn it.

We teach rational thinking directly as well as by example. Children can learn to think in precise, analytic fashion when given the encouragement to do so and the "methodology." They can learn how to formulate goals, how to question what they are told, how to establish a logical hierarchy of values, and the means of relating to others in rewarding ways.

Teaching rationality by example speaks for itself: If the parents are not rational, they cannot hope to impart reasoning to their children. The first rule for all of us as parents should be to work on our own rationality. But as we all know too well, this isn't easy. We all act without thought some of the time, and it can be difficult to pick up the indications of our irrationalities. This is one more situation in which communication between parents can help. We can usually uncover the irrationality in someone else's position easier than in our own, and they can see the flaws in our thinking. Not that husbands and wives should sit in judgment on one another. Far from it. But by discussing issues at length and developing their lines of communication, they can each refine their thinking and assist one another in eliminating faulty thinking and emotionally motivated conclusions.

Teaching rational thinking to our children calls for a lot of free communication and exploration of ideas. At all times, we try to emphasize the following:

1. *The highest value in life is living.* We want our children to learn to value themselves above all other values, to see their own personal happiness as important and good, and worth working for. We teach them to reject any notion of worthlessness, of being bad or sinful by nature. We want them to understand that acting toward others with justice is important to their own life and the world in which they want to live, and that they owe responsibilities to others, in justice, just as others owe responsibility toward them. But we teach them to reject any philosophy which holds that the purpose of one's life is to serve others in a life of sacrifice, a philosophy which says, "I am of no value; my life has purpose and meaning only if I 'pay my way' by living it for others."

2. *Rational thinking is directed toward responsible behavior.* Responsible behavior is behavior which is directed toward goals which make life rewarding. Irresponsible behavior is behavior which frustrates the attainment of our goals. It is self-defeating and self-destructive. If a child

does "what he feels like doing" with little consideration of how it will affect his ultimate goals, he is behaving in an irrational and irresponsible manner. If he behaves in ways which ignore the rights of others, he is acting irrationally since he is helping to create a world which will be less than satisfying to him, a world in which others will violate his rights. We try to show the children how irresponsible behavior results from irrational thinking. We try to avoid that tiresome business of saying, "You should have known better." It is more effective, we have found, to help them understand what they were thinking and where they may have gotten off the track of rationality, and how this led to self-defeating behavior.

3. *We teach them to avoid magical thinking.* We try to teach them that life is not determined by luck; they make their own luck. We want them to learn to *question,* to accept no answers which violate their reason, and to reject any suggestion that "blind faith" is an explanation. We want them to grow up with confidence in their own ability to solve problems, achieve goals, and reach an understanding of the world in which they live, relying on their own intellect and the evidence of their senses rather than on myths, superstitions, and "fate."

4. *Setting goals and systematically working toward them is essential if life is to be other than chaotic.* Living every day as it comes with little thought of the future is a little like wandering the halls of a building blindfolded during an earthquake: The roof may fall in on you. Parents have learned this and we want to teach it to our children. When they are young, we set the goals for them and teach them how to achieve them. With experience in achieving goals and the rewards they bring, they learn to set further goals. By talking to them in terms of life goals, dreams, aspirations, we reinforce the value of becoming a goal-oriented person. By teaching them to critically examine their various options, we teach them how to achieve the goals they choose.

5. *Through discussion of examples, we teach them how*

to evaluate the rationality or irrationality of a position. We teach our children to be "judgmental." Teaching a child to take no stand, to "judge not, that ye be not judged," is not conducive to the development of rationality. We want them to learn to evaluate, make judgments, and be willing to be judged. The mental meandering represented in a situation ethic in which there are no absolutes, no blacks and whites, only grays, and in which every opinion is considered as valid as every other, is an abdication of responsibility and a statement of a lack of self-esteem. If our child says, "My teacher said something very stupid today," we are not going to tell him, "You mustn't talk that way about your teacher; it's not your place to pass judgment on what she tells you: She's the teacher." It is very much his place to judge the logic of any statement and to evaluate the behavior he observes. If we teach him otherwise, we are encouraging him to *not* think. We teach our children that *expressing* their judgments in the classroom and elsewhere may work to their disadvantage and would, therefore, be irrational, and that making judgments doesn't mean criticizing others, but yes, by all means evaluate, and their home is the best place for exchanging views and evaluations, and the best place for developing a sound, rational set of values and ethics.

6. *Emotions are desirable. Life without emotion would be dead. But unless we control emotions rather than being controlled by them, life can become intolerable to us and those with whom we interact.* Emotions are to living what flavoring is to a meal. But emotions are somewhat like water flowing from a faucet. We want to teach our children they would not be *controlling* the flow if they welded the valve shut. Nor would they be controlling it if they removed the valve and permitted the water to gush freely. The message we hear so often today is "Let it all hang out." Adults gather in romper rooms like sensitivity groups and adolescents confront their teachers in free-swinging rap sessions. "Say it like you feel it" is the word. "Kick, scream, and swear, but make sure you don't hold

anything in; it's bad for you to suppress your gut feelings." Following such "reasoning" to its illogical conclusion would force us to conclude that infancy is psychologically the healthiest period in life—perhaps the only one!

The young child acts on his emotions; his feelings provide the motivation for his actions. As he matures—if he matures—his motivation comes from a rational analysis of his desires. They become his goals and he sets out to do those things necessary to achieve them. Not that he doesn't "feel." Of course he feels. He just doesn't let his feelings determine his actions or get in the way of his reaching his goals.

What our children will hopefully learn from us is that emotions are good. They are taught that through thinking and acting in rational and responsible ways, they can experience rewards which will bring positive feelings. He can thus "control" his feelings, i.e., bring them about, through his choice of actions. We teach them that feelings are feelings, neither good nor bad. That feelings and thoughts are nothing to be ashamed of, and that experiencing an emotion, any *emotion*, and *acting* on the emotion is a matter of choice. We try to teach them how to make choices which will not be counter to their self-interest nor against the interests of others.*

Parents have a power which is today largely dormant. They have been told the world is a madhouse in which only the inmates offer the promise of sanity by surrender to a collective madness. They have been told to accept a collective guilt for all ills of the society, to beat their breasts, use only the first-person plural, never first-person singular, and admit to one's worthlessness. Turn all ra-

---

* We might wish the scope of this book permitted us to go into a full exposition of rational thinking and the teaching of rationality to our children. It is, without reservation, the most important education we can provide for our children. We do suggest two books we have found helpful: *A Guide to Rational Living* by A. Ellis and R. Harper (Prentice-Hall 1961), and *The Psychology of Self-Esteem* by N. Branden (Nash Publishing, 1969).

tional values upside down. Applaud trash as art, filth as beauty, violence as legitimate social protest, chemical alteration of the brain as "mind expansion." And above all, they have been told any deviation from the tribal mores of the robots, any attempt to assert and value individuality, is a crime against the society. Free will, psychologist B. F. Skinner tells us, is a myth; freedom is a "luxury" we can no longer afford. Is it any wonder so many parents have struck their colors and surrendered to propagandists and their children? If we join in their surrender, we can expect to become slaves, fellow inmates in their asylum. And we shall hand our children over to a life of intellectual, emotional, and moral vacuity. Our power as parents is there. So is the responsibility. Acceptance of this power and responsibility is the challenge of the seventies.